WAFFEN SS
An illustrated history

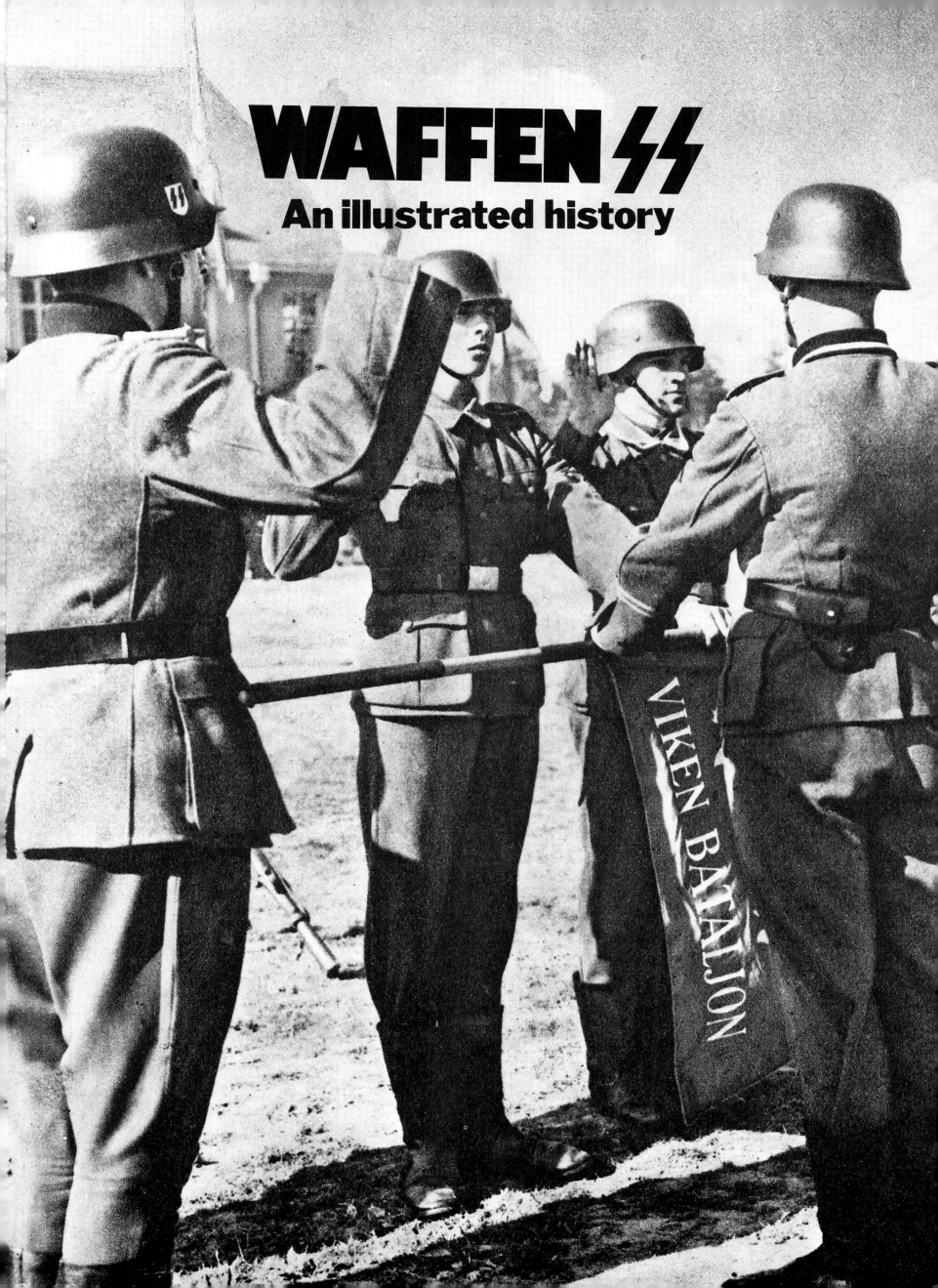

WAFFEN ⚡⚡

An illustrated history

Adrian Gilbert

GALLERY BOOKS
An imprint of W.H. Smith Publishers Inc.
112 Madison Avenue
New York, New York 10016

Published by Gallery Books
A Division of W H Smith Publishers Inc.
112 Madison Avenue
New York, New York 10016

Produced by
Brompton Books Corp.
15 Sherwood Place
Greenwich, CT 06830

ISBN 0-8317-9286-8
Printed and bound in Spain by Gráficas Estella, S.A.
Printed in Spain

10 9 8 7 6 5 4 3 2 1

Page 1: Norwegian volunteers to the Waffen SS swear the
oath of allegiance on their battalion colors.
Page 2: Armed with an MG34 machine gun, troops of the
Polizei Division await the order to fire.
Page 3: An SS guard for the Protector of Bohemia and
Moravia stands to attention.
This page: The Leibstandarte 'Adolf Hitler' goose steps down
the Wilhelmstrasse in front of Hitler and other leading Nazis.
The Leibstandarte, in their function as Hitler's special guard,
acted as Nazi Germany's ceremonial troops on occasions of
state.
Pages 6-7: Surrounded by SS security men Hitler is greeted by
an adoring crowd.

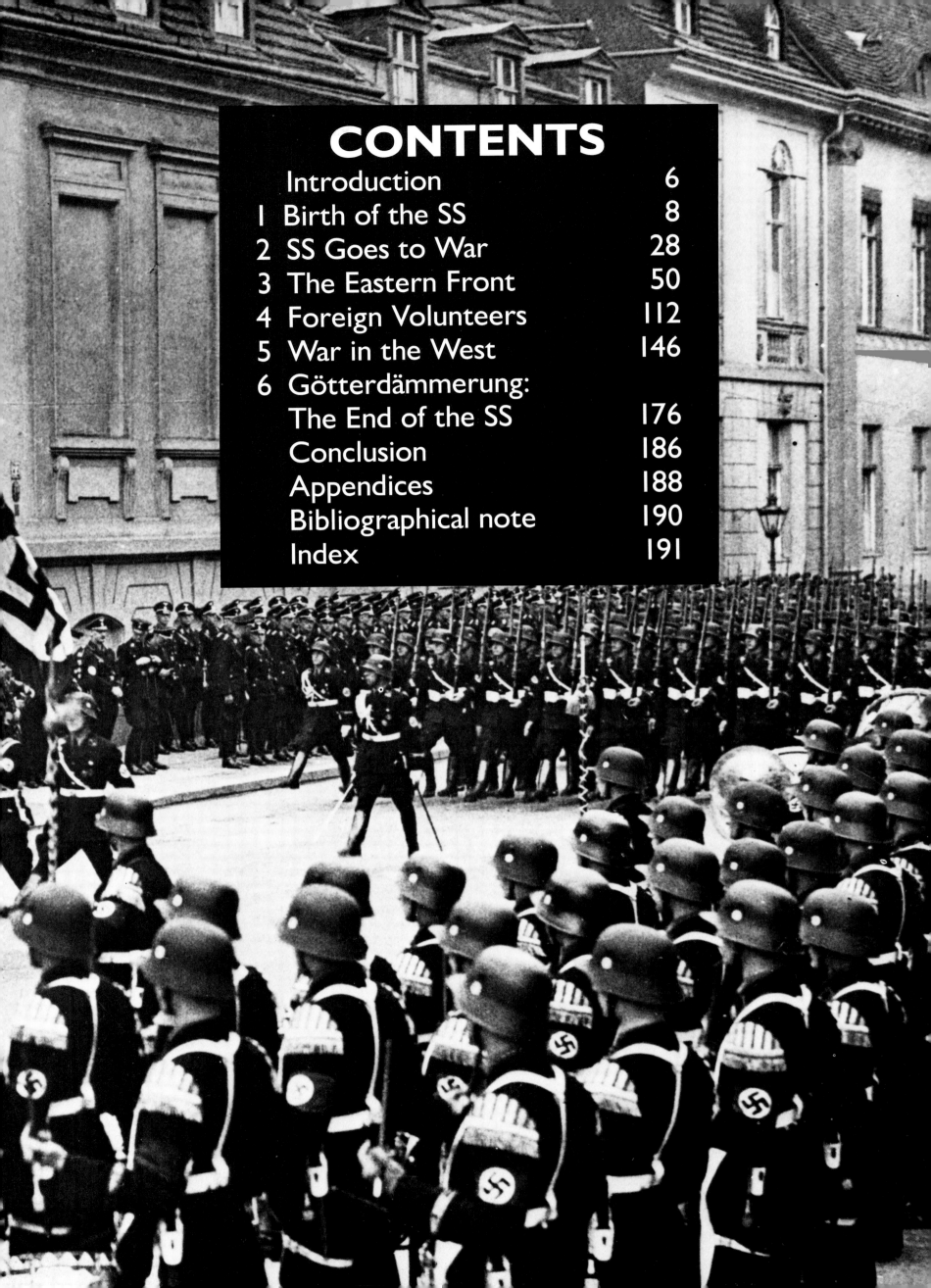

CONTENTS

INTRODUCTION

O f the many acronyms, initials and abbreviations which have become a commonplace of life in the twentieth century, the two letters 'SS' have acquired a baleful association with terror and dread. Even before World War II the SS had become identified, to the world at large, with the more odious aspects of Hitler's Germany, but the revelations that followed the discovery of the concentration camps were profoundly shocking. Yet despite the persistent interest in and morbid fascination for the SS, confusion abounds as to what it was and what it did.

The formal origins of the SS (Schutzstaffel or protection squad) date back to 1922 but its genesis lay in the collapse of governmental authority after Germany's defeat in World War I. Immediately after the armistice of November 1918 Germany was thrown into turmoil; a period which saw the rise of the Freikorps, bands of right-wing ex-soldiers who fought for control of the streets against communist and other left-wing groups. The Freikorps' philosophy of *bierkeller* violence and parochial political intrigue acted as a seed bed for the development of the SS. Even in later years, when the SS had acquired a veneer of quasi-respectability, its roots remained embedded in the world of the Freikorps.

During the 1930s the organizational elements within the SS began to develop; some with distinct, separate functions, others less so, but all remaining a part of the SS 'empire.' The Allgemeine (general) SS represented the original SS, some stalwarts claiming membership back to the early 1920s, but by the end of the next decade it merely comprised those members who were not a part of the other branches. Strutting about in black full-dress uniforms the men of the Allgemeine SS were the embodiment of the public image of the SS, but once war was declared they were dispersed to other sections, reduced from around 250,000 to little over 40,000.

The decline of the Allgemeine SS was compensated for by a dramatic increase in a key area of SS activity, the takeover and rationalization of Germany's police forces and security service. In 1931 Himmler had set up his own security organization, the Sicherheitsdienst or SD which, under the control of Reinhard Heydrich, emerged as the official German security and intelligence service in 1938. At the same time, Himmler was fighting for control of the various police forces in the Third Reich. Outmaneuvering his opponents he was appointed Chief of Police in 1936 and set about reorganizing the system into two main branches: the Ordungspolizei (order police) – abbreviated to Orpo – and the Sicheitspolizei (security police) – Sipo – which was itself divided into the Reich Kriminalpolizei (state criminal police) – Kripo – and the infamous Geheime Staatspolizei (state secret police) – Gestapo. Heydrich was assigned control of the Sicheitspolizei, a command he combined with the SD in September 1939 to form the powerful new aggregation called the Reichssicherheitshauptamt (main office of state security) or RSHA. As the war progressed so too did the power and influence of the RSHA, the organization responsible for the enslavement and destruction of millions of people in German-occupied Europe.

As a direct consequence of the activities of the RSHA came the expansion of the concentration camp system, manned by another branch of the SS, the Totenkopfverbände (death's head detachments). Alongside the torturers of the Gestapo and the roving bands of Einsatzgruppen death squads from the RSHA, the concentration camp guards represented humanity at its very lowest. The last important element within the SS was the Waffen (armed) SS itself – the subject of this book.

Birth of th

e SS

The origins of the SS go back to the early 1920s, when the Nazi leader Adolf Hitler felt the need to supplement his brown-shirted SA (Sturmabteilungen or storm groups) with a small personal bodyguard, which later became known as the SS (Schutzstaffel or protection squad). In marked contrast to the brawling street thugs of the SA, the SS was intended to be a tightly knit, highly motivated organization which would act as the spearhead for the Nazis' rise to power. Throughout the 1920s, the SS grew from an original nucleus of 200 men in 1923 to a force of 52,000 a decade later. Although the leader of the SS – Heinrich Himmler, appointed Reichsführer SS on 16 January 1929 – was determined to increase the power and prestige of his organization, the rapid influx of recruits during 1932-33 became a problem in itself. Sensing a Nazi victory at the polls, 'undesirable' opportunists jumped on the SS bandwagon; exacting standards were breached and the SS began increasingly to resemble the SA. Consequently Himmler imposed a temporary ban on new membership and promptly sifted out unsuitable material.

When the Nazis took power in 1933 the need for an *armed* bodyguard to protect the new German Führer became paramount. Accordingly, on 17 March 1933 Hitler ordered the formation of a headquarters guard under the command of his old personal bodyguard and chauffeur Josef 'Sepp' Dietrich. In this *Stabswache* (staff guard) of just 120 specially selected SS personnel lay the genesis of the Waffen SS.

In September 1933 these latterday guardsmen received the official title of Leibstandarte SS 'Adolf Hitler' and on 9 November they swore a solemn oath which bound them, unconditionally, to the Führer – and to him alone. At a stroke Hitler had created a new praetorian guard which stood outside the demands and interests of the state, ready instead to slavishly obey the commands of its 'emperor'. Kitted-out in dramatic black full-dress uniforms, the men of the Leibstandarte escorted Hitler during his official functions and acted as his guard at the Chancellery.

The Leibstandarte was not the only armed SS unit, however. During 1933 and 1934 SS 'political action squads' were set up in a number of major cities throughout Germany and, organized along lines similar to that of the Leibstandarte, they were given the title of SS Verfügungstruppe (SS-VT) and quickly grew to a size of two standarten (regiments). The third element in the armed SS evolved from the guards who ran the rapidly expanding system of political prisons and concentration camps. Known by their appropriately sinister title of SS Totenkopfverbände (death's-head detachments), they were commanded by the notorious Theodor Eicke.

The first test for the SS came with the elimination of the SA. Once in power, Hitler had dropped the revolutionary rhetoric of the Nazi Party's street-fighting days, whereas the SA radicals in the Party wanted to push things further in a program that would have included the replacement of the German Army by an SA militia. Horrified at the prospect, the Army promised its full support for Hitler in exchange for the monopoly of the 'right to bear arms' and for the crushing of the SA as a political force in Germany. Keen to prove themselves and to gain the ascendancy over their SA rivals, Himmler's armed SS made ideal executioners.

In the weeks following 30 June 1934, while the secret police rounded up unsuspecting SA leaders (including its chief Ernst Röhm), the execution squads of the SS killed their former political comrades in arms. The 'blood purge' of 1934 was a turning point for the SS; they were now the undisputed 'political soldiers' of the Reich, elevated to the status of an independent organization within the Nazi Party by Hitler's decree of 26 July 1934. Ironically, the Army's price for the ending of the SA threat included the acceptance of the SS as a separate armed force. Although the SS appeared to pose no threat to the Army's pre-eminent position in 1934, Hitler's decree sowed the seeds of a bitter rivalry between the two organizations.

The recruitment policies of the SS during the 1930s placed great importance on maintaining racial purity: extensive documentation of a sound Aryan pedigree was essential for the successful recruit. Standards of physical excellence were equally important and evidence of any minor medical complaint would be enough to bar the applicant. In an attempt to break down the traditional class barriers that were such a feature of the German Army, the SS encouraged recruits from all social backgrounds and formal educational qualifications were dispensed with. This last factor caused problems in the recruitment of suitable officers so that, for example, before 1938 around 40 percent of entrants to the officer cadet schools had only an elementary school education. Consequently the professional qualities of some SS officers were found wanting. Despite this, the war was a great teacher and by 1942 complaints leveled against SS military skills were few and far between.

In keeping with the exacting standards of fitness required by the SS, athletics, organized sports and other forms of physical exercise formed an integral part of the recruit's training program. Officers and other ranks undertook sporting activities together, a practice which emphasized the unity and comradeship of all ranks within the SS – in marked contrast to attitudes in the Army at that time.

Another special feature of SS training was to make it as realistic as possible. Thus, alongside the athletics field was the assault course where the young recruit was subjected to a form of battlefield indoctrination only just short of the real thing. The use of live ammunition was standard and at times included complete artillery barrages. As this was one of the most

Above: **The military band from the Standarte 'Deutschland' takes part in one of the melodramatic torchlight parades so beloved of the Nazis, 8 May 1936.**

Right: **The high tide of German expansion, October-November 1942. The Waffen SS participated in most of Germany's great victories from this period; only in the conquest of Norway and the campaigns in North Africa was the SS absent. The twin defeats at El Alamein (October-November 1942) and Stalingrad (November 1942-February 1943) marked the turning of the tide; from then on Germany was forced onto the defensive.**

Below right: **Obergruppenführer Felix Steiner – not only the most important single influence behind the development of the dynamic tactical theories adopted by the SS, but an excellent field commander in his own right.**

devastating experiences a raw soldier could undergo, a controlled bombardment was an invaluable method of inuring him to the realities of war. Himmler was particularly enthusiastic about this new approach and, according to American historian George Stein, the SS leader noted: 'Every man became accustomed to his weapons and also to being within 50 to 70 meters of the explosions of his own artillery fire.' Such realistic training inevitably led to casualties, which Himmler accepted as unfortunate but necessary, as 'every drop of blood spilled in peacetime saved streams of blood' once the real fighting began.

This radical training program was largely instigated by the two officer training schools at Bad Tölz and Braunschweig, institutions which produced many of Germany's top fighting commanders. Alongside the emphasis on physical fitness and realistic combat conditions, SS training encouraged the display of initiative — at all levels of command, from the most junior NCO upwards — and the development of intelligent and flexible methods of teamwork in a variety of tactical situations. This combination was very much a part of the German military tradition — the Sturmtruppen (assault groups) of World War I, for example — and during World War II the crack SS (and Army) formations further improved upon the system.

Two leading figures were largely responsible for the impressive training and organization of the SS. Paul Hausser, a retired lieutenant general from the Reichswehr, was appointed an SS Brigadeführer in 1934 and given the task of organizing and training the SS-VT. Hausser later became a distinguished wartime commander, the only SS general to command an army group. Felix Steiner was responsible for the development and implementation of the new tactical theories within the SS. Under Steiner's command, the SS Standarte 'Deutschland' became a showpiece regiment for others to emulate.

Despite such stringent preparation for battlefield conditions, the armed SS remained a part of Himmler's secret empire and as such were the 'political soldiers' of the Reich. While the other three services of the armed forces occasionally displayed less than total enthusiasm for the Führer's crackpot theories, the SS were steadfast upholders of Nazi ideology, whatever it entailed. They relished the total obedience required of them as Hitler's bodyguard, their motto was, *Meine Ehre heisst Treue* — Loyalty is my Honor.

Sudetendeutsche Männer

können sich zur Aufnahme in die SS-Verfügungstruppe (Leibstandarte-SS „Adolf Hitler" und die SS-Standarten „Deutschland", „Germania", „Der Führer"), in die SS-Totenkopf-standarten und in die Polizei (Schutzpolizei, Geheime Staats- und Kriminalpolizei) melden

Auskunft erteilen die Annahmestellen und jede Polizei- und Gendarmerie-Station

Above: **Standing within the confines of Dachau Concentration Camp outside Munich, Reichsorganisationleiter Robert Ley (fourth from left) inspects work in progress with his entourage, 2 November 1936. Fourth from right (with ceremonial dagger) is Theodor Eicke, a Nazi bully-boy who had been appointed head of the concentration camp system in 1934. Eicke subsequently became commander of the 'Totenkopf' Division.**

Left: **A 1939 recruitment poster issued by the SS, appealing to ethnic Germans of the Sudetenland (then a part of the German Reich) to join one of the various sections of the organization – the Verfügungstruppe, the Totenkopf Standarten or the police.**

Himmler saw the SS as a modern reincarnation of the chivalric orders of the Middle Ages and even went as far as instituting an Arthurian Round Table, complete with spurious coats of arms for favored officers who met regularly in the Reichsführer's castle at Wewelsburg. Daggers and signet rings were also provided as coveted symbols of SS exclusiveness. And when a man became a fully-fledged member of the SS he took more than a simple step from recruit to soldier; rather, he was transformed as an individual, moving from one life to another. The process was completed with a mass initiation ceremony, involving torchlight parades and a binding oath to Hitler.

When Hitler formally reintroduced conscription and decreed the expansion of the Army on 16 March 1935, he also issued an order for an increase in size of his armed SS forces, which then comprised the Leibstandarte, the two standarten ('Deutschland' and 'Germania') of the SS-VT and the Totenkopfverbände. The latter units were not recognized as 'soldiers' by the Army (which controlled the conscription system), a decision which caused continuing controversy in Army-SS relations when the Army refused to acknowledge membership of death's-head detachments as military service. Nonetheless the Totenkopfverbände became a major area of SS expansion during the 1930s: the five sturmbanne (battalions) of March 1936 had grown to a force of four standarten (each of three sturmbanne) with supporting units by 1 April 1938. Alongside their peacetime duties, supervising the concentration camp system, the Totenkopfverbände would, in wartime, have a supplementary role, acting as a general reserve for the SS-VT. Thus, contrary to claims made by Waffen SS apologists, there was a direct connection between the Totenkopfverbände and the other elements of the armed SS. During the war the movement became a two-way process with Waffen SS troops being sent (albeit in limited numbers) to help run concentration camps.

While Eicke, the ambitious leader of the Totenkopfverbände, was keen to improve the quality of his sturmbanne, they were in no way comparable to the elite troops of the rest of the armed SS. This distinction remained until the disbandment of the Totenkopfverbände, although the 'Totenkopf' Division went on to distinguish itself during the fighting on the Eastern Front.

Himmler would have liked to dramatically expand the armed SS as a whole but Hitler moderated his demands in the face of determined Army opposition. The Army remained a powerful force in German political life until the Blomberg-Fritsch scandal of January 1938, which allowed Hitler to undermine the power of the generals by taking direct control of a newly created command structure (Oberkommando der Wehrmacht – OKW) over that of the Army High Command (Oberkommando des Heeres – OKH). This humiliation for the Army was followed by the annexation of Austria in March 1938. Shortly after, a new SS-VT standarte, 'Der Führer', was raised, largely from Austrian recruits. By 1939 the SS-VT consisted of four standarten (including the Leibstandarte) with full supporting arms, including two motorcycle battalions along with communications and pioneer battalions. As the threat of war became ever more certain during the summer of 1939, the nucleus of an elite SS fighting force had emerged.

Left: **A trio of top Nazis, from the left: Kurt Daluege (subsequently head of the German police force), Heinrich Himmler (head of the SS), and Ernst Röhm (head of the SA). By the time this photograph was taken (August 1933) the antipathy between the SS and the SA was becoming marked. In less than a year Röhm would be dead, murdered by the SS, the power of the SA severely curtailed.**

Above left: **The spawning ground for the Nazi bully-boy – right-wing, ex-Freikorps thugs adopt Nazi swastikas at a rally in Munich, March 1923. Although the SS prided itself on having developed a certain degree of refinement and discipline – that is, relative to the absolute loutishness of the SA – it was in fact sustained by the same violence that had characterized the Nazi movement from the beginning.**

Above: **The massed ranks of the SA Brown Shirts are deployed alongside the black of the SS at a Nuremberg rally. The theatrical showcase for Nazi ideology, the Nuremberg rallies also broadcast to the world the growing importance of the SS after the Night of the Long Knives, 30 June 1934.**

Above: **Leading members of the Nazi hierarchy at an early Nuremberg rally in 1927. From the left, they include Himmler, Rudolf Hess, Gregor Strasser, Hitler and Karl von Pfeffer-Wildenbruch (subsequently a police general and commander of the 4th SS Polizei Division).**

Right: **Recruits to the SS *Begeitkommando* of the Leibstandarte 'Adolf Hitler' undergo the rigors of early morning drill, April 1933. Beside being raised as a combat élite, the Leibstandarte was called upon to perform ceremonial duties, hence the strict attention to 'square bashing.'**

Above: **An early member of an SS unit, photographed in a typically 'heroic' pose. During the 1920s SS uniform was broadly similar to that of the SA, but after 1934 it began to develop along increasingly military lines.**

Left: **SS street-fighters pose with a stand of flags and placards captured from German communists. The SS may have been primarily a bodyguard for Hitler, but this did not stop them from engaging in 'freelance' street-fighting activities such as Jew-baiting and the beating up of communists and other left-wingers.**

Below left: **SS recruits, wearing simple fatigues, collect their midday meal. Although the leaders of the SS were keen to play down the military possibilities of their organization in order not to arouse the suspicions of the Army, SS recruits were trained along strict military lines.**

Above: **Hitler takes the salute during a march-past of the Leibstandarte 'Adolf Hitler,' 30 January 1938. Standing by Hitler's car are Hess (on the left), Sepp Dietrich (commander of the Leibstandarte) and Himmler.**

Left: **A line-up of the 1st Company of the Leibstandarte, prepared for inspection. As Hitler's guardsmen they were nicknamed the 'Asphalt Soldiers,' a reflection on their attention to parade-ground drilling. On the left of the photograph is Theodore Wisch, then a company commander but subsequently the CO of the Leibstandarte Division.**

Left: **Hitler inspects SA and SS men at the 1934 Nuremberg Rally. Himmler, the Führer's ever-present companion at such events, stands second from the right.**

Above: **A carefully composed shot of the color party of the Leibstandarte 'Adolf Hitler' underneath one of the giant eagles at the Luitpold Arena, Nuremberg.**

Left: **SS recruits train on a power-mounted quadruple 2cm Flak gun. While the Luftwaffe was responsible for handling the larger-caliber antiaircraft guns, all German divisions had a substantial AA component of their own.**

Below: **An SdKfz 8 schwerer Zugkraftwagen 12t of the heavy artillery of the Verfügungstruppe advances over a hillock while on maneuvers. The SdKfz 8 was designed as an artillery tractor, capable of towing all the various types of field guns used at divisional level.**

Right: **A young artilleryman on the Verfügungstruppe looks through his stereoscopic range-finder. The '2' on his collar insignia denotes that he is part of Standarte 'Germania,' one of the three standarten that made up the SS-V Division.**

Left: Under the watchful eye of his examiners an Unterscharführer displays his climbing skills with ice ax and crampons. A major area of SS expansion lay in the number of its mountain divisions, a total of six by the end of the war. Accordingly, mountain training schools were set up to develop the special skills required of mountain troops. For the most part the SS mountain divisions were deployed in the Balkans in antipartisan duties; and the mountainous terrain encountered in this region placed sound climbing techniques at a premium.

Left: Flemish recruits' musketry skills are examined by SS officers on the rifle range. By carefully positioning the rifle on the tripod-mounted sandbag the examiner is able to tell how accurately placed a potential shot will be. They are using the 7.92mm Karbiner 98k, the standard infantry rifle used by German armed forces during World War II.

Above: **Totenkopfverbänden recruits are given instruction in the use of the Karbiner 98k.**

Left: **Two SS artillerymen chalk a facetious comment onto a 15cm shell, presumably intended for use against the British as the umbrella and top hat symbols are references to the British Prime Minister Neville Chamberlain.**

Left: **SS troops at a sports day ceremony. The cult of the Aryan body was a central tenet of Nazi ideology, and physical exercise was taken seriously by the SS. Certainly, it helped produce first-class troops able to withstand the physical rigors of campaign life.**

Below: **In a German hospital, war disabled are encouraged to take part in sporting activities as part of their rehabilitation program. In this group are men from the Army and Air Force as well as the SS, the latter identifiable by the SS runes on his sports vest.**

Above: **One of the high spots in an SS man's career, the award of his ceremonial dagger. This was a special distinction given only to graduates of the officer training schools at Bad Tölz and Braunschweig.**

Left: **Beside the outdoor pursuits of the athletics track, rifle range and field exercise ground, SS officers were also expected to demonstrate a high level of tactical competence. Here, NCO aspirants conduct a sand-table exercise at one of the officer-training academies.**

Above left: **Hitler salutes an SS motorcycle detachment as it rides through the streets of Nuremberg. Although at a peacetime propaganda rally, these troops would soon be committed to war.**

Far left: **The color guard of the Leibstandarte 'Adolf Hitler' parades through the streets of Vienna in March 1938, following the Anschluss – the Nazi takeover of Austria and its incorporation into the Greater German Reich.**

Left: **Troops of the Leibstandarte talk to Nazi supporters in the Sudetenland, the German-speaking area of Czechoslovakia taken over by the Germans after the treaty of Munich, September 1938.**

Above: **Troops of the Standarte 'Deutschland' hold back cheering crowds on the arrival of Mussolini in Germany during 1938. From the Nazis' rise to power in 1933, the two totalitarian states of Italy and Germany had grown closer together: the Anti-Comintern Pact of 1936 was followed by a formal alliance, the 'Pact of Steel,' in May 1939. Such alliances inevitably helped to divide Europe into two armed camps, the democratic West against the Axis states of Italy and Germany. During the final years of peace, Germany's rearmament program carried on apace, a process that included the steady expansion of the Waffen SS.**

SS Goes t

o War

As dawn broke on the morning of I September 1939, German troops marched over the border into Poland, the first move in what would become World War II. Few in numbers, the troops of the armed SS would necessarily play only a limited role in an otherwise Army operation. Nonetheless the campaign would provide the units involved with invaluable battle experience.

The SS were split up among the regular Army formations dispersed along the projected invasion front; the Leibstandarte SS 'Adolf Hitler' (supported by the SS combat engineer battalion) was attached to General von Reichenau's Tenth Army; SS Standarte 'Deutschland' (with the SS artillery regiment and SS reconnaissance battalion) joined Major General Kempf's 4th Panzer Brigade; SS Standarte 'Germania' became a part of the Fourteenth Army under General List. The third SS-VT standarte, 'Der Führer,' was not yet fully trained and consequently did not take part in the invasion of Poland. Although 'Germania' remained in reserve for most of the four-week campaign, 'Deutschland' received a heavy baptism of fire at the Battle of Brest-Litovsk. The Leibstandarte had a particularly hectic time, for after fighting in the south of Poland it was transferred to the 4th Panzer Division, battling its way to Warsaw, before participating in the encirclement maneuver of the Battle of the Bzura.

Despite the fighting commitment of the SS, their conduct during the campaign was widely criticized in official Army circles. The main charge was the disproportionately heavy casualties suffered by SS units compared with those of the Army which, the Army claimed, was a consequence of poor leadership. In 1939 the majority of SS officers and NCOs did indeed lack the military skills of their Army equivalents, but they countered these accusations by claiming that in order to operate effectively on the field of battle, SS units must be organized into full divisions, commanded by their own officers. Despite the usual bitter Army opposition, Hitler was persuaded to allow the SS to do just that for the forthcoming campaign in the West.

The expansion of the Waffen SS (the title 'Waffen SS' became official in February) during the pause before the invasion of France and the Low Countries in May 1940 brought the Leibstandarte up to the strength of a reinforced regiment – and subsequently to that of a brigade in August. The SS-VT was formed into a full division (SS Verfügungsdivision or SS-V), under the command of Paul Hausser. At the same time a number of Totenkopf standarten were grouped together to form a division, while a third division, formed mainly from Ordungspolizei personnel (Germany's para-military police) strengthened by cadres of SS-V and Totenkopf troops, also came into being. Led by the old Nazi stalwart Karl Pfeffer-Wildenbruch, the Polizei Division was very much a second-line formation, so that while the other Waffen SS divisions were generally well-equipped and fully motorized, this formation was organized as an infantry division, equipped with Czech weapons.

The campaign in the West would establish the fighting reputation of the Waffen SS and, the reverse side of the coin, an often callous disregard for the terms of the Geneva Convention which was to become a hallmark of SS operations throughout the war.

Right: **The famous 'panzer corridor' which severed the Allied line and isolated the main bulk of the French Army in the south from the Allied troops to the north. The 'Totenkopf' Division was dispatched to support the XVth Army Corps (5th and 7th Panzer Divisions) and was involved in the British counterattack around Arras on 21 May. After their successes in the Netherlands, the Leibstandarte 'Adolf Hitler' and the Verfügungsdivision followed along in the wake of the panzer breakthrough in France and became part of the force pushing the Anglo-French armies northward to the Dunkirk perimeter.**

Below right: **Firing a Czech-made 7.92mm ZBvz 30 light machine gun, SS troops support an infantry attack in France. Designated as the MG 30(t) by the Germans, this was an excellent weapon (the basis of the British Bren gun), and large stocks were confiscated in the German takeover of Czechoslovakia.**

Below left: **The Polish campaign of September 1939, showing the exploitation of the German attack and the Soviet Union's own offensive into the eastern half of Poland. SS troops took part in the race toward Brest-Litovsk, the encirclement battle on the Bzura around Kutno and the drive on Warsaw.**

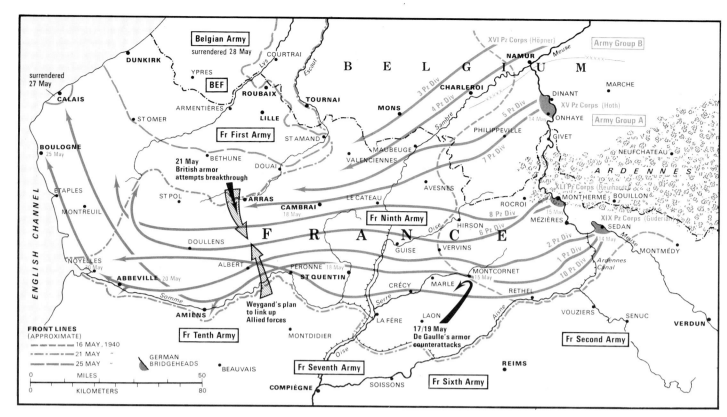

Hitler's invasion plans were postponed on numerous occasions, but finally the date was set for early May 1940. The Leibstandarte and SS Standarte 'Der Führer' (detached from the SS-V Division) were deployed on the Dutch frontier, ready to race across the border to secure the many vital river and canal crossings prior to the main German advance. The rest of the SS-V Division was stationed near Munster, its role to exploit the initial breakthrough into Holland. The 'Totenkopf' Division was held in central reserve by the Army High Command (OKH) while the Polizei Division was deployed further back still, behind the Rhine.

The Leibstandarte and the forward units of the SS-V Division had little difficulty in overrunning the Dutch positions as the German armed forces invaded Holland on 10 May 1940. The SS columns raced through Holland, so that by 14 May advanced units were on the outskirts of Rotterdam. The following day the Dutch surrendered and, wasting no time, the motorized SS were swiftly re-deployed southward for the main battle against the French and British.

On 16 May the 'Totenkopf' Division was sent into action in support of Rommel's 7th Panzer Division, which had cut a swathe across southern Belgium and eastern France. On 21 May, however, both divisions were thrown into disarray when a British counterattack smashed into the German flanks. Panic broke out in some 'Totenkopf' units, but eventually the British assault was held and the following day the attackers were thrown back. By now the German advance had divided the Allied forces into two, with large numbers of British, French and Belgian troops separated from the main bulk of the French Army to the south of the 'panzer corridor.' The forward German units turned 'right' to eliminate the Allied forces in the north and the Leibstandarte, SS-V and 'Totenkopf' were in the forefront of the advance.

Right: **Obergruppenführer Theodor Eicke, who led the 'Totenkopf' Division in France in 1940 and in the Soviet Union from June 1941 until his death in action on March 1943.**

Below: **Once the campaign in Poland was over, the bulk of the German armed forces was transported westward for the impending invasion of France and the Low Countries, but substantial SS forces remained behind to administer the newly-occupied territory. In this photograph a Waffen SS soldier inspects a group of orthodox Jews, 1939-40. From the outset the Germans imposed the most brutal regime over their Slav subjects and the country's large Jewish population was singled out for 'special treatment.'**

Above left: **A section of SS men from the Standarte 'Germania' (embroidered on the cuff title of the soldier on the right) takes cover behind a farmhouse somewhere in France. The trooper on the left carries the legs of a mortar over his shoulder and is armed with the old 9mm P 08 Luger automatic pistol. Although withdrawn from service the Luger remained a popular possession among German (and Allied) troops.**

Above right: **Amidst the inferno of war, a motorcycle team of the Leibstandarte 'Adolf Hitler' negotiates a burning town.**

While the Leibstandarte and SS Standarte 'Deutschland' distinguished themselves in fiercely contested canal crossings, a unit of the 'Totenkopf' Division committed one of the first recorded SS atrocities. After being held up and taking heavy casualties from a British battalion (the 2nd Royal Norfolks), the commander of a company ordered captured British troops to be lined up against a wall and machine-gunned. Altogether, 100 men of the Norfolks were killed. Although attempts were made to bring the company commander, Obersturmführer Fritz Knochlein, to justice, the affair was hushed up until after the war, when two badly wounded survivors of the massacre testified against Knochlein in a trial which led to his execution in 1948.

As the Germans advanced, the Allies were compressed into an ever-decreasing pocket, eventually centering around Dunkirk. The Leibstandarte was heavily engaged in the fighting around the village of Wormhoudt, an action which nearly cost unit commander Sepp Dietrich his life when he was trapped in a burning ditch in No Man's Land for several hours as the battle raged about him. After the capture of Wormhoudt a further atrocity was committed, this time by Leibstandarte troops who, under the command of Wilhelm Moncke, killed 80 British prisoners of war in cold blood. Moncke, however, escaped Knochlein's fate and lives as a retired businessman in Hamburg, despite renewed charges being laid against him.

Hitler's famous 'stop order' led to the cessation of ground hostilities before Dunkirk. Yet again the SS were re-deployed, this time to deal with the French Army which was holding a line along the River Somme. Operating alongside the German Army's panzer divisions, the SS motorized units had little difficulty in smashing through the French lines on 6 June. As the French forces became progressively demoralized so the speed and depth of the German advance increased. The Leibstandarte led the SS advance and within two weeks had linked up with the Army Panzers as far south as Vichy. On 17 June the newly formed French government under Marshal Pétain decided to sue for peace and on the 22nd the armistice came into effect. The war in the West was over: the Waffen SS had won its spurs.

Left: **Kitted-out in black full-dress uniforms, these SS men sit about in a well-known Danzig café in the last few weeks before the outbreak of war. Formerly an important German seaport on the Baltic, Danzig had become a Free City as a result of the Versailles Treaty of 1919, a decision which affronted German national sensibilities and which was cleverly exploited by the Nazis for their own ends. The movement of thousands of German Nazi supporters – ostentatiously calling themselves 'tourists' – into Danzig in August 1939 was intended to increase tension between Poland and Germany and to install key military personnel who would be ready for action once fighting broke out.**

Right: **Again masquerading as 'tourists,' SS troopers in Danzig inspect port facilities from the fashionable Zoppot pier. These men were a part of Totenkopf Sturmbann 'Gotze,' a paramilitary SS police unit intended to aid German military operation.**

Below left: **An armored car of the 'Heimwehr Danzig' provides support for German troops in securing the city at the onset of hostilities on 1 September 1939.**

Below: **Beyond Danzig, 'Heimwehr' troops set a brisk pace in support of Army operations aimed at cutting through the 'Polish corridor.'**

Above: **Making good use of an old cart for protection, SS troops return fire against Polish positions in this all-but-ruined town. Despite being totally outmaneuvered by the German armed forces, isolated units of the Polish Army fought with their customary bravery, so that in tactical situations such as this – the reduction of a small town – the Germans had to work hard to secure the objective.**

Below: **Carefully advancing behind a SdKfz 232 armored car, SS troops of the Leibstandarte 'Adolf Hitler' approach a burning town center; the Polish defenders have been forced to retreat in the face of superior German firepower. The white cross on the rear of the armored car was a specific recognition device for the Polish campaign.**

Above: **An infantry section of SS troops prepares to dig in while holding forward positions on a patch of open ground within the central area of this Polish town. The men of the Leibstandarte 'Adolf Hitler' fought a whirlwind campaign, being transferred from one battle zone to another in the space of a few weeks.**

Above: **Even though the Western Allies
called Hitler's bluff when he declared war
on Poland, they were unable to stop him
overrunning the country in a mere five
weeks. Hitler's victory was a major feat
of German arms, and it was one which
included the contribution – albeit small –
of the Waffen SS. Here, a grateful Führer
congratulates Sepp Dietrich, commander
of the Leibstandarte, for his unit's part in
the campaign. Behind Dietrich stands
Max Wünsche, later to become a
renowned Waffen SS panzer
commander.**

Left: **A carefully posed picture of a
machine-gun team of the Ordungspolizei
holding a rooftop position in a battered
Warsaw. They are armed with the
obsolete MG08 machine gun, a pre-World
War I weapon indicative of the inferior
allocation of weapons to most SS units at
that time; it was only after 1942-43 that
the SS began to receive the pick of the
German arms industry.**

Left: **Armed with a 9mm MP38 sub-machine gun, plus stick-grenades in his belt, this Oberscharführer of the SS – VT Standarte 'Germania' leads his men along a roadside on the Western Front, May-June 1940.**

Above: **A grim-faced motorcycle unit pauses in its drive through a French town as the great attack begins. In all probability these men belong to the divisional reconnaissance battalion, which in the German armed forces was a heavily armed unit that advanced well to the fore of the main body and was capable of fighting for tactical intelligence if necessary.**

Above right: **Dutch civilians look on as SS troopers discuss the situation during the initial stages of the German invasion of the Low Countries. They are wearing the famous SS camouflage smock, an item of kit first derided by the German Army but subsequently copied by it.**

Right: **Crouching down by the roadside the crew of a 3.7cm Pak 36 antitank gun prepares for a possible Allied counterattack. Even by the standards of 1939-40 the Pak 36 was inadequate when faced with medium or heavy tanks; along with the infantry gun of the same caliber SS troops derisively named it the 'door-knocker'!**

Above: **SS infantrymen rest alongside a line of German panzers on a French road. The tanks in the foreground are PzKpfw IIs, while on the far left is a PzKpfw I.**

Right: **Sited in carefully prepared positions, as part of a training exercise, troops of the Polizei Division bring up ammunition in readiness to fire an 8.1cm Granatwerfer 34 – the standard German mortar assigned to infantry during World War II.**

Envisaged as élite assault troops, the armed **SS** paid considerable attention to overcoming one of the chief natural obstacles in land warfare – rivers. Whereas the passively minded French relied heavily on the defensive qualities of their major waterways, the Germans were successfully developing riverine assault tactics.

Left: **A practice run – a pontoon section on two inflatables is used to carry a 7.5cm IGI8 light infantry gun over to the opposite bank.**

Above: **Under fire, SS troopers paddle furiously to make the return journey to pick up more men and supplies.**

Right: **Although the negative has suffered from the ravages of time, this picture nevertheless conveys the dangers of river crossings: suffering from a leg wound, an SS trooper is ferried away from the combat zone by his comrades.**

Above left: **An interesting picture of Obergruppenführer Paul Hausser, commander of the SS-VT Division, writing orders with staff from Standarte 'Germania.' The presence of a captured British soldier (in background) suggests that this photograph was taken as the SS pushed northward, eventually toward the Allied perimeter at Dunkirk. Unlike the British prisoners who were murdered by SS troops at Le Paradis and Wormhoudt, it would appear that this soldier awaits evacuation to a PoW camp.**

Above: **Racing forward at speed, this SS trooper dashes across a roadway, as infantry and motorcyclists attempt to maintain the momentum of the advance.**

Left: **Veterans of the first few weeks of fighting in France, these troops of the SS-V Division prepare to move out of a farmyard. Typical of combat infantry at this stage of the war, they are well-equipped with stick-grenades and boxes of ammunition for the section MG34 machine gun, better known to the Allies as the 'Spandau.'**

Left: **Wounded, weary and unshaven, NCOs from the SS-V's Standarte 'Deutschland' look across to enemy positions in the distance. Later to become the 2nd SS Panzer Division 'Das Reich,' the SS-V Division demonstrated its combat abilities in a variety of situations during the course of the campaign.**

Above: **Armed with antitank rifles SS troops stand to attention. Antitank rifles were an oddity of the early stages of World War II, although they were employed by most of the major combatants. The German Panzerbüchse 39 fired a hardened steel or tungsten-cored 7.92mm bullet which could penetrate up to 25mm of armor plate at 300 meters. As tank armor increased, however, antitank rifles became progressively less effective and, in fact, were rarely used by the Germans after 1940.**

Above: **Troops from the Standarte 'Germania' of the SS-V Division allow themselves the luxury of a standing meal break during the campaign in the West. After the French campaign, 'Germania' was given the responsibility of acting as the core for an entirely new division, comprising troops from Western Europe as well as Germany.**

Left: **SS troops carried out mundane military duties alongside their more glamorous roles, including the essential task of mine clearance. While one soldier (right) is equipped with a mine detector, his companion (left) stands watch with the old police weapon – an MP34 sub-machine gun. The third member of the team removes a mine.**

Above right: **Troops of the Polizei Division carry a soldier wounded in the leg; their exhaustion is clearly evident. Although kept in reserve for most of the campaign, the division was given its chance in the final stages and acquitted itself more or less creditably.**

Right: **A snapshot found on the body of an SS soldier killed during the opening stages of the war against the Soviet Union; it shows a group of 'Totenkopf' troops celebrating their success in the 1940 campaign in France.**

Right: **SS tankmen act as an escort guard for Adolf Hitler himself, on the Führer's visit to Hendaye on the French-Spanish border. There, Hitler hoped to persuade General Franco to join the Axis partnership, but the Spanish dictator wisely refused to be drawn. Although this practice was not to last long, tank crewmen wore an extra-large black beret – covering a lightweight leather helmet – which can be seen in the photograph.**

Below: **The parades which celebrated German victory in the West were many if not particularly varied. This one shows Leibstandarte 'Adolf Hitler' troops receiving the thanks of the citizens of Berlin. The time between the Fall of France (summer 1940) and the invasion of the Balkans (spring 1941) would represent the only real period of 'peace' for the field formations of the Waffen SS.**

Right: **The refusal of the British to come to terms with Germany came as a surprise and Hitler ordered his generals to prepare for the invasion of Britain. A number of SS units were assigned to the proposed invasion force and were instructed in rudimentary amphibious techniques: here, an SS 3.7cm Pak 36 antitank gun is loaded onto an 'invasion' barge. Hitler, however, began to lose interest in the scheme and the RAF's victory in the Battle of Britain during the late summer and autumn of 1940 signaled the end of the invasion plan.**

Above: **France 1940 – Sepp Dietrich at another awards ceremony for the victors of the Leibstandarte 'Adolf Hitler.' Dietrich has the ribbon for the Iron Cross (Second Class) attached to the second button of his tunic and wears the Iron Cross (First Class) on his left breast pocket, which also holds his Nazi Party membership badge and wound and combat badges.**

Left: **As a general reward for its conduct during the campaign in France and the Low Countries, the Leibstandarte was awarded this standard at a ceremony in Metz, September 1940.**

The Easte

rn Front

The armistice of 22 June 1940 brought the fighting in France to a conclusion, but the conflict between the German Army and the SS over recruitment continued unabated. At the outset of war, SS recruitment was centralized under the control of SS Brigadeführer Gottlob Berger, an organizational genius obsessively devoted to the expansion of the SS. From the beginning, Berger saw the Army as his main enemy and he employed any and every device to get past OKW's recruitment restrictions. In addition to the authorized yearly quota, Berger had two other sources of manpower: firstly, young German volunteers who could be inducted into the SS before reaching military service age and, secondly, racially suitable volunteers from beyond the confines of the Reich and consequently outside the OKW recruitment system. Despite the appeal of serving in a dashing and successful organization such as the Waffen SS, there were simply not enough German youths to fulfill SS requirements. Fortunately for Berger, Germany's conquests in Europe had opened up a new reservoir of Volksdeutsche (people of German descent) and other 'acceptable' Aryan nationalities ('Germanics') such as the Dutch and Scandinavians. Berger wasted no time in sending his recruiting officers in search of the right material.

The increase in SS numbers brought forward the development of a new command structure to reflect the importance of what was gradually becoming a new combat arm to be set alongside that of the Army. On 15 August 1940, Himmler authorized the formation of the SS Führungshauptamt (SSFHA) which was in effect a 'High Command' comparable to that of the Army's OKH. At the time, Himmler claimed the SSFHA was merely an organizational device for those SS units not under the direct control of the Army (as they would be when in the field), but in spite of his protestations, this was yet another move to further the progress of the SS.

In keeping with the general increase of Germany's armed forces in preparation for the forthcoming invasion of the Soviet Union, the Leibstandarte 'Adolf Hitler' was uprated to a brigade (then a full division once the invasion was underway) while a completely new division was authorized. The leadership of the new division was drawn from existing formations, as were specialist units and SS Standarte 'Germania' from the SS-Verfügungsdivision, but the bulk of its personnel came from Germanic volunteers. Initially called 'Germania', the formation was soon renamed SS Division 'Wiking' and under this designation became one of the best divisions in the SS order of battle. To make up for the loss of one of its standarten, the SS-V was assigned a Totenkopfstandarte and renamed SS Division 'Reich' (subsequently 'Das Reich').

Always a source of reinforcement for the main field units, the Totenkopfstandarten were reorganized to play a more active role as independent formations. Thus, Kampfgruppe 'Nord' was formed from two standarten (plus artillery and other support units). Previously, another 'spare' Totenkopfstandarte had been dispatched to an outpost within Norway's Arctic Circle and after reinforcement became SS Infantry Regiment 9. The five remaining Totenkopfstandarten were transported to the major SS training grounds at Debica in Poland, where they were re-equipped and redesignated as SS infantry regiments. Lastly, the Totenkopf cavalry units were reorganized to become SS Kavallerie Regiments 1 and 2, the

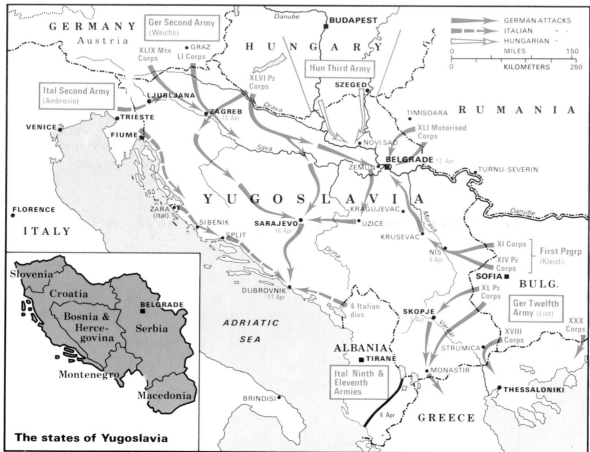

The states of Yugoslavia

Left: **The German invasion of Yugoslavia was planned in a matter of days but its execution was a model of ruthless efficiency. The 'Reich' Division distinguished itself when a reconnaissance detachment captured the capital, Belgrade, within a week of the start of the offensive. Once under Axis control, the Germans set about exploiting the regional differences within Yugoslavia, a country created by the Versailles settlement of 1919 and not so much a nation state as a loose and often unfriendly confederation.**

Left: **Standartenführer Otto Kumm, a good example of the officer who rose to prominence through the SS and who embodied the fanaticism of that type of SS soldier. A veteran of the Eastern Front, Kumm commanded Standarte 'Der Führer' of the 'Das Reich' Division at the Battle of Kharkov and subsequently went on to command the 'Prinz Eugen' Division.**

Above: **SS infantry, supported by an SdKfz 222 armored car of the Leibstandarte 'Adolf Hitler,' engage in a firefight with Soviet troops in a town in the Ukraine, August 1941.**

nucleus of the 8th SS Kavallerie Division 'Florian Geyer'.

Now that the Totenkopfstandarten had been elevated to combat status (and formally become members of the Waffen SS), their previous duties were taken over by the Ordungspolizei (police units under Himmler's direct control, although not part of the Waffen SS). Responsible for the brutal subjugation within the occupied countries of Central and Eastern Europe, the Ordungspolizei expanded rapidly – like so many other institutions of Nazi repression – to a figure of between 25 and 30 regiments with full support units.

* * *

After the fall of France, the next target for German conquest was Great Britain, but the failure of the Luftwaffe to overcome the RAF during the Battle of Britain increased Hitler's reservations about the entire project. Despite the German-Soviet Non-Aggression Pact of 1939, Hitler's enmity for Soviet Russia was one of the constant factors in his strategic outlook and in the closing months of 1940 his thoughts began to turn eastward – to the destruction of the communist state. On 18 December 1940 he issued *Fall Barbarossa*, the directive for the invasion of the Soviet Union. During the spring of 1941 the German war machine prepared itself for the impending struggle, but events elsewhere led to the SS moving south rather than east.

Italy, Hitler's ally in the Pact of Steel, had launched a surprise attack against Greece; but as so often happened with Mussolini's adventures, plans went awry and the Italian Army suffered a succession of humiliating defeats at the hands of its Greek opponents. Before Operation Barbarossa could go ahead, Hitler was concerned that his southern flank be secured – especially as the British were sending reinforcements to the Greeks – so German forces were redirected to bail out the Italians. The plan of campaign was suddenly expanded when the Yugoslav government, which had previously been bullied into allying itself with the Axis powers, was overthrown and a new anti-German administration put in its place. Enraged by this turn of events Hitler ordered the destruction of Yugoslavia 'with merciless brutality.'

On 6 April 1941, Germany invaded Yugoslavia and Greece. The Yugoslav Army was no match for the veterans of the Blitzkrieg and SS Division 'Reich' was in the forefront of the invasion plan, a detachment under SS Hauptsturmführer Fritz Klingenberg audaciously capturing the capital city of Belgrade on 13 April. Greece was considered more of a problem and List's Twelfth Army was assigned to its conquest. The SS forces in Greece consisted of the Leibstandarte 'Adolf Hitler,' which became involved in a series of hard-fought battles against Greek, British and New Zealand troops. Among those engagements was the capture of the Klissura Pass – held by a strong Greek detachment – that entered SS folklore as an example of direct leadership. The reconnaissance battalion, under the command of Kurt Meyer, was given the task of securing the Pass but the advance became bogged down in the face of fierce Greek resistance and a small group under Meyer's direct command found itself pinned down in a hollow on the mountainside. Determined to get the attack going again, Meyer hit upon the dramatic expedient of dropping a primed hand grenade behind the last man in the group. 'Never again,' he subsequently related, 'did I witness such a concerted leap forward . . . The spell is broken. The hand grenade has cured our lameness.' Klissura Pass was taken along with 11,000 prisoners and the award of a Knight's Cross for Meyer. On 27 April, Athens fell to the Germans and by the end of the month the campaign was effectively over, the Leibstandarte being ordered north to Prague to refit for the assault on Russia.

The Waffen SS took part in all of Germany's campaigns in Europe but it was in the fatal struggle with Soviet Russia that Himmler's legions found their apotheosis. As the cutting edge of Nazi ideology it was inevitable that the SS should find itself in the forefront of the war against the antithesis of fascism. The brutal nature of the war was increased further by the Nazi belief that Slavs were 'Untermensch' (sub-humans). Thus the citizens of the Soviet Union – like those of Poland and Yugoslavia, for example – were not accorded the status of human beings and were to be exploited as slaves of the German Reich until they dropped or, if they proved troublesome, to be destroyed out of hand. Atrocities became the order of the day on both sides and all elements of the SS, including the Waffen SS, became experienced practitioners of indiscriminate killing.

As dawn broke on the morning of 22 June 1941, Hitler ordered his armed forces to invade an unsuspecting Soviet Union. Although caught totally by surprise, the Soviet Union accepted Hitler's challenge of a struggle to the death, and for the next four years the world was to witness the greatest war in history in which the forces involved numbered millions, as indeed did the casualties.

The German deployment stretched from the Baltic to the Black Sea and was organized into three army groups: the SS Division 'Totenkopf' and SS Polizei Division were assigned to Army Group North (with SS Kampfgruppe 'Nord' and SS Infantry Regiment 9 operating out of Finland); SS Division 'Reich' to Army Group Center; and Leibstandarte SS 'Adolf Hiltler' and SS Division 'Wiking' to Army Group South. A statistical report made at the time revealed the combined strength of the Waffen SS to be 160,405 men (see Appendix III), the bulk of which was distributed among the frontline divisions.

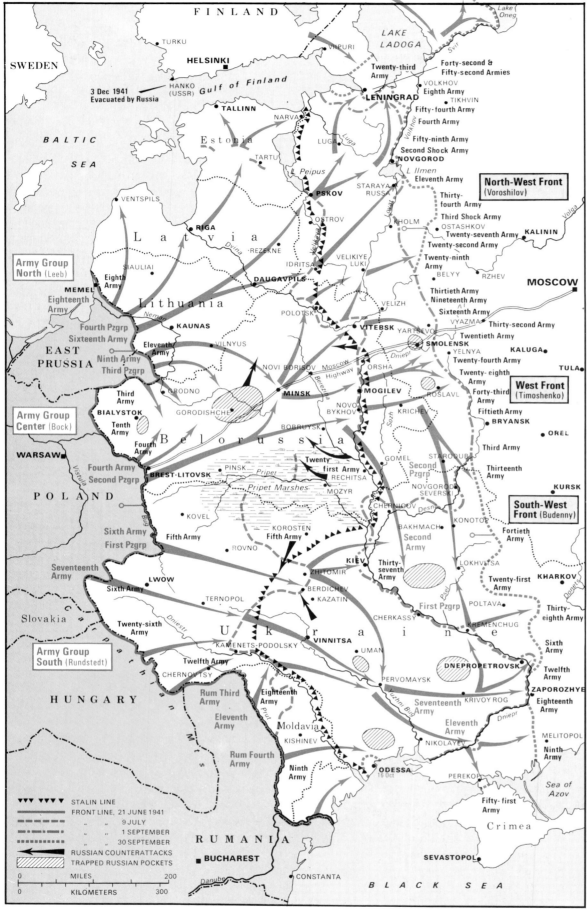

Left: **Operation Barbarossa, the German invasion of the Soviet Union, 22 June – 30 September 1941. In the north, 'Totenkopf' was operating with Hoeppner's Fourth Panzer Group, the Polizei Division in reserve; in the center 'Reich' was part of Guderian's Second Panzer Group; in the south 'Wiking' and Leibstandarte 'Adolf Hitler' were deployed alongside the tanks of Kleist's First Panzer Group.**

Below: **In addition to fighting in the front line, Waffen SS troops were used in rear-area operations. Here, Russians ('snipers' in the original caption) are rounded up alongside a disabled Soviet tank by a Waffen SS police unit.**

Exploiting their initial advantage of surprise the German armored columns advanced deep into Soviet territory with the Leibstandarte and 'Wiking' divisions impressing their Army counterparts with their aggression and skill in attack. SS Division 'Reich' distinguished itself on numerous occasions and, renamed 'Das Reich', it came within a few kilometers of Moscow during the final, faltering stages of the operation to secure the Soviet capital, which marked the end of the great German offensive of 1941. Completely exhausted, the Germans found that their Blitzkrieg techniques – breathtakingly successful elsewhere – had met their match in the vast expanse of the Soviet Union and against the extraordinary stamina of the Red Army. The force of the Soviet counteroffensive during the winter of 1941-42 shocked the German Army High Command, which argued for full-scale withdrawals. They were, however, overruled by Hitler who ordered his armies to stand fast, which in retrospect probably proved a sound military decision. In this phase the Waffen SS divisions added to their

reputation as dashing troops in attack with a new steadfastness in defense.

The only real SS failure occurred in the far north on the Finnish Front when SS Kampfgruppe 'Nord' was ignominiously routed in an engagement on 2 July 1941. Although it was temporarily divided up among the other units by an exasperated Army commander, Himmler persevered with 'Nord' so that a few months later it was overhauled and, following reinforcement, was upgraded as a division – ultimately as the 6th SS Gebirgs (Mountain) Division 'Nord.'

As the campaign season opened in the spring of 1942 the German High Command planned a major offensive through southern Russia to the oil-rich Caucasus region. During the course of the year the SS divisions – still suffering from the battles of the previous winter – were withdrawn and refitted with a strong tank component plus assault guns and armored personnel carriers. In November 1942 Leibstandarte, 'Das Reich', 'Totenkopf' and 'Wiking' were redesignated as SS panzergrenadier divisions and were now equal in terms of equipment to many full panzer divisions in the Army.

Hitler was increasingly impressed with the combat record of his 'political soldiers' and ordered the formation of the 8th SS Kavallerie Division 'Florian Geyer' in September 1942 and of two new German-recruited panzer grenadier divisions (9th Panzergrenadier Division 'Hohenstauffen' and 10th Panzergrenadier Division 'Frundsberg') in December. This expansion, combined with the massive replacement losses of the other divisions, went far beyond the OKW quotas but Hitler's direct support forced the Army to make concessions. Berger, the desk-bound warrior of the SS Hauptamt (main office), had triumphed over the Army. Statistics presented by George Stein revealed the extent of the SS victory: Waffen SS troops in the field numbered 141,975 on 1 September 1942 (with a further 45,663 in training and reserve), while on 1 September 1943 the figures had virtually doubled to 280,000 and 70,000 respectively.

The great German offensive of 1942 had begun well, but the failure to capture Stalingrad and the Soviet Union's own offensive (launched on December 1942) were to prove disastrous for the Germans. By early 1943 General Paulus's Sixth Army was totally isolated in Stalingrad and was forced to surrender on 2 February. Other substantial German forces in the Caucasus region also faced the grim possibility of being cut off by the speed and depth of the

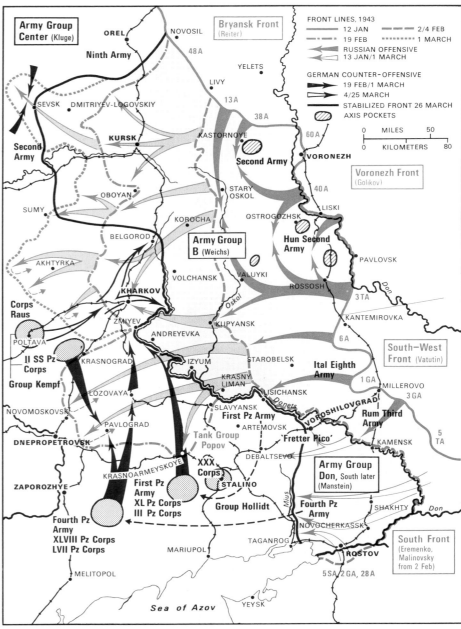

Soviet penetration. Although Field Marshal von Manstein, commander of Army Group South, managed to extricate his forces from the Soviet trap, the momentum of the Soviet advance prevented him from stabilizing the line. By mid-February 1943, however, Manstein sensed that the Soviet thrust had become dangerously over-extended and he launched a timely counter-attack in the Kharkov region. This threw his opponents into complete disarray and allowed the Germans time to restore order to their positions in the south.

The formations spearheading the assault on Kharkov (captured on 15 March) were the three divisions of the newly formed SS Panzer Corps (Leibstandarte, 'Das Reich' and 'Totenkopf') under the command of Paul Hausser. For the first time a substantial body of Waffen SS troops had fought together and the result had been a resounding victory. To Hitler, who was increasingly disillusioned by repeated Army failures and what he saw as a defeatist attitude among his generals, it was a godsend. From then on the Waffen SS became one of the Führer's special concerns, to the delight of the SS soldiers in the field who now received the pick of the latest weapons and equipment.

The period after the German recapture of Kharkov was relatively quiet, as both sides prepared to resume hostilities in earnest in the summer. The Soviet salient around Kursk became the focus of operations: the Germans planned to eliminate the salient altogether, while the Soviet High Command saw it as a useful springboard from which to launch its own summer offensive. The unimaginative German plan consisted of two major thrusts, one each side of the salient. This, however, had been anticipated by the Red Army, which had prepared a carefully sited in-depth defensive screen to blunt the German attack. On 5 July the Battle of Kursk began, with Hausser's SS Panzer Corps deployed on the southern flank. The Germans made reasonable progress in the first few days, particularly in the south, but the nature of the war had changed and greatly improved Red Army forces held the German thrusts before counter-attacking themselves. The SS Panzer Corps again fought well, although weakened by the removal of the Leibstandarte to bolster German forces in Italy following the Allied invasion of Sicily on 10 July.

The German failure at Kursk lost them their chance to regain the strategic initiative on the Eastern Front and from then on they were forced to react to Soviet moves. For the rest of 1943 the hard-pressed Germans fell back westward across the Soviet Union, relinquishing ground only as a means of preventing a Soviet breakthrough. The elite SS divisions, redesignated as full panzer divisions, acquired a new role as Hitler's 'fire brigade,' sent from one danger area to another as the situation demanded. The decisiveness with which both 'Das Reich' and 'Totenkopf' were employed in throwing back Soviet assaults earned them repeated praise from those generals who had them under their command. In November the Leibstandarte returned to the Eastern Front and, re-equipped with large numbers of the latest Panther tanks, it fought with Army panzer divisions to crush a Soviet armored corps and retake Zhitomir.

While the men of the Waffen SS were locked in battle on the Eastern Front, Hitler continued to authorize the formation of new SS divisions. Short of volunteers, the SS recruiters began to enforce various forms of conscription and a substantial part of both the 'Frundsberg' and 'Hohenstauffen' divisions were drafted from the older members of the Hitler Youth. This idea was developed further with the formation of the next elite German division: authorized in January 1943 it was activated in July and designated the 12th SS Panzergrenadier Division 'Hitlerjugend'. In March 1943 the 11th SS Freiwilligen-Panzergrenadier Division 'Nordland' was created from Norwegian and Danish volunteers.

Below: **Primitive, cetainly; effective, possibly – a section of SS soldiers negotiates a river within the pine forests of the northern sector of the Eastern Front.**

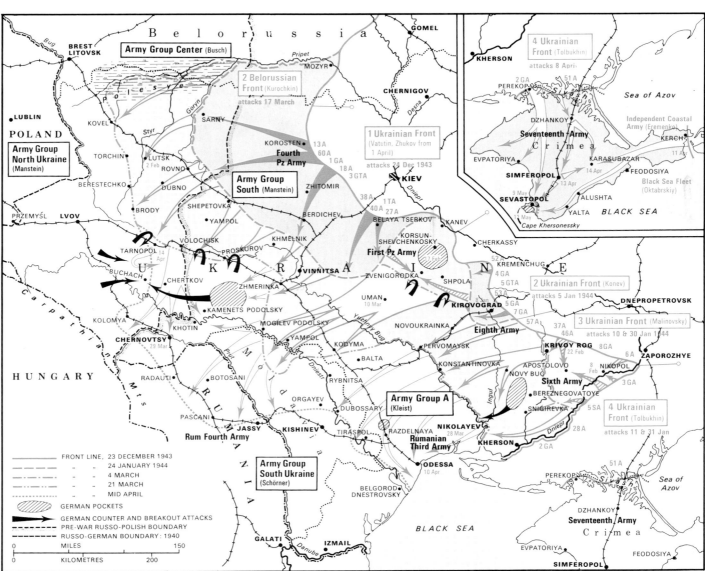

Above left: **Combat-hardened panzer crew members stand beside their tank, taking a brief rest from the rigors of battle.**

Above right: **The Soviet winter offensive of 1943-44 took the form of a massive blow in the south which cleared the Ukraine by April 1944. The SS were particularly hard-pressed in the defense of the Ukraine: 'Wiking' spearheaded the breakout from the Korsun-Cherkassy pocket, while the Leibstandarte and part of 'Das Reich' received help from 'Hohenstaufen' and 'Frundsberg' in the breakout from the Kamenets-Podolsky pocket.**

The German positions on the Eastern Front underwent a dramatic deterioration when, on 14 December 1943, the Soviet Union launched another massive offensive in the Ukraine – a non-stop battle which lasted until mid-April 1944, culminating in the expulsion of the Germans from the Soviet Union in the south. The speed of the Soviet advance led to the encirclement of large numbers of German troops. The 5th SS Panzer Division 'Wiking' and SS Brigade 'Wallonien' were caught in the Korsun-Cherkassy pocket amid the remains of two army corps. As the Soviet forces began to press in on the perimeter of the pocket, the specter of another Stalingrad hovered over the German High Command.

Hitler eventually gave permission for the encircled troops to attempt a breakout. 'Wiking' spearheaded the attempt. There followed a week of intense fighting (from 12-19 February) in which 'Wiking' lost all its heavy equipment and up to half of its personnel but succeeded in smashing a way through to safety. The second encirclement was the Kamenets-Podolsky pocket, containing the First Panzer Army with the Leibstandarte and elements of 'Das Reich.' In order to save the First Panzer Army Hitler allowed the SS reserve – the 9th and 10th SS Panzer Divisions – to attempt a breakthrough to the pocket. Recently arrived from 'forming up' in France the two SS divisions succeeded in breaking through the Soviet lines to allow the encircled forces enough time to escape.

The battered Leibstandarte and 'Das Reich' battle groups were sent westward to refit and prepare for the expected Anglo-American invasion; the former went to Belgium while the latter joined the rest of the 'Das Reich' division in southern France. The 'Hohenstauffen' and 'Frundsberg' divisions were based in Poland in anticipation of another Soviet attack, along with the unfortunate 'Wiking' (now reduced to 4000 men), while the long-serving 'Totenkopf' remained in front-line service in the East.

Having barely recovered from their winter mauling, the Red Army struck again on 13 July 1944 and ripped the German Army Group Center apart. Once again the SS panzer divisions were thrown into the breach: 'Wiking' and 'Totenkopf' (plus the Army's 19th Panzer Division) repulsed the Soviet assault on Warsaw during August, while in the Balkans the backbone of the German defense was provided by nominally second-grade SS units withdrawn from their usual antipartisan warfare duties. By the end of 1944 the situation on the Eastern Front was desperate. The Balkans were lost and Soviet troops were laying siege to the Hungarian capital, Budapest, while to the north the Soviet armies were massing on the borders of Germany in preparation for the last great offensive against Berlin. Worn down and exhausted, the remaining Waffen SS formations would prove unable to stem the tide.

Left: **CO of the Leibstandarte, Sepp Dietrich (right), holds a conference with the general commanding mountain troops in Greece. In the background is Max Wünsche, still acting as Dietrich's ADC.**

Below: **Captured Greek troops are led into captivity past a group of Leibstandarte armored cars. On the left stand two SdKfz 222 armored cars, the one to the rear converted to a command vehicle (with frame aerial); on the right is an SdKfz 232 (Fu) radio vehicle, again with frame aerial.**

Right: **The Allies had hoped that Greece's rough terrain and poor communications would slow the German advance; once again, however, German Blitzkrieg tactics overcame these obstacles, so that forward units of the Leibstandarte tore through the Anglo-Greek defenses within days. Here, men of the Leibstandarte unload equipment and weapons after crossing the Corinth Canal. In the foreground is a 5cm Pak 38 antitank gun.**

Above: **Secure in victory, SS troops drive past a crowd of Greek peasants, some of whom have thought it prudent to give the Nazi salute. The swiftness of the German drive through Greece took the civilian population by surprise and opposition was correspondingly slight. Later, however, the combination of a tradition of fierce nationalism and the brutality of the German occupation led to the development of a well-supported resistance movement. As the war progressed increasing numbers of SS troops would be deployed in the Balkans to suppress the various resistance movements.**

Below: **On entering a Greek village, Dietrich stops to question curious Greek inhabitants. The essential function of motorized formations, such as the Leibstandarte, was to break through the enemy's forward defensive line and drive deep into his territory, thereby preventing any chance of recovery. Intelligence gained from local sources could be vital in this sort of warfare.**

Left: **While the Leibstandarte fought in Greece, so the 'Reich' Division took part in the invasion of Yugoslavia. Here, 'Reich' troops take advantage of local waterborne transport to ferry themselves along the Danube to secure their objective: the Yugoslave capital itself.**

Right: **A convoy of SS troops pauses during a triumphal march-past through the streets of Belgrade. The capture of the Yugoslav capital was the result of a daring feat of arms brought off by a small assault group from 'Reich's' reconnaissance battalion under the leadership of Hauptsturmführer Fritz Klingenberg. By using a motorboat Klingenberg was able to slip through the city defenses and force its surrender from a bewildered and confused mayor.**

Above: **Despite their seeming maneuverability, motorcycle combinations were vulnerable to the age-old enemy of mobility – mud. In this case, the rider attempts to steer a steady course while his comrades provide extra power.**

Right: **Sturmbannführer Fritz Witt plans the assault on the Klidi Pass. The pass was an important link in the Allied defenses and in securing their objective the Leibstandarte suffered relatively heavy casualties – including Witt's younger brother, Franz.**

Above: **The number of shells being brought out to serve this gun illustrates the intensity of the SS bombardment of Allied positions around the Klidi Pass. The artillery piece is a 15cm FH18 heavy field howitzer, the largest piece of ordnance at the direct disposal of the Leibstandarte, capable of firing a 43.5kg shell to a maximum distance of 13,250m.**

Right: **An explosion rents the air as an SS machine-gun crew dives for cover. Although the German armed forces made spectacular progress during the opening stages of Operation Barbarossa, the Red Army fought back with a resolution that came as a surprise to SS veterans used to the easy victories in the West against France.**

Far right: **Dugin against the possibility of a Soviet counterattack, this SS trooper looks across typically flat terrain to a burning Russian village on the horizon.**

Above: **An NCO of an SS reconnaissance unit grins for the camera during the early stages of the great advance into Russia. He is armed with a Soviet 9mm PPSh sub-machine gun, a robust weapon used in vast quantities by the Red Army during World War II – and popular with SS troops too.**

Right: **A group of SS men secure the services of a local translator to explain the legend on this recently captured Soviet flag which reads: 'Fight for Lenin and Stalin – be prepared!' The company commander on the right of the photograph is Hauptsturmführer Hugo Kraas, who later rose to become the last commander of the 'Hitlerjugend' Division.**

Above: **Although not a 'first wave' formation, the Polizei Division did not have to wait long before being sent into combat as part of Army Group North. In this photograph Polizei troops take a breather alongside a ruined house near the town of Luga.**

Right: **Standing in well-constructed entrenchments Polizei soldiers man a radio transmitter, one of the essential devices for battlefield communication. The Polizei Division cuff title is clearly visible in this photograph, although unusually these troops are wearing the standard SS collar insignia instead of the army pattern usually worn by police troops.**

Top: **The sheer size of the Russian steppe is visible here as German motorcycle combinations advance eastward, a pall of smoke rising from the horizon as the grasslands burn.**

Above: **A German tank narrowly misses being hit as it moves forward against a Soviet stronghold.**

Left: **An MP40 sub-machine gun slung over his shoulder, an SS NCO leads two Red Army tankmen away from their disabled T-34. The straw scattered across the tank was intended for purposes of camouflage – when fighting on the defensive a well-concealed tank can wreak havoc on armor advancing across an exposed position.**

Below: **A motorcycle combination drives through the smoldering ruins of a Soviet village, which the retreating Russians had set fire to as part of their 'scorched earth' policy during 1941. Even at this early stage of the campaign, signs of exhaustion can be seen on the faces of these SS soldiers.**

Above: **Sturmbannführer Kurt Meyer, his recently awarded Knight's Cross hanging from his neck, directs operations during the opening stages of the invasion of the Soviet Union. Meyer was a notable representative of the type of commander who rose from within the SS itself: aggressive and charismatic in equal measure. At the age of 33 he was appointed to the command of the 'Hitlerjugend' Division, thereby becoming the youngest divisional commander in the German armed forces.**

Right and above, far right: **Two photographs from a sequence showing troops from the 'Wiking' Division moving up to secure a town in southern Russia. Although the Standarte 'Germania' – transferred from the 'Reich' Division – was a veteran unit, the other elements of the division consisted of new recruits drawn from Scandinavia. That 'Wiking' performed so well during its first campaign suggested that troops drawn from outside Germany's borders might be an effective way of fulfilling the SS's manpower requirements. Certainly, the invasion of the Soviet Union marked the beginning of a vast expansion of foreign recruitment.**

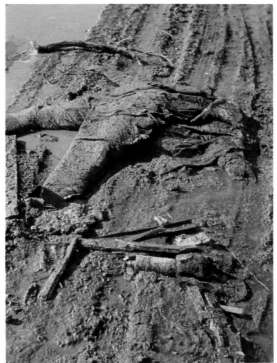

Left: **The squashed body of a soldier lies flattened in the road, one of the many victims of the seemingly inexorable German thrust into the Soviet Union. The period from 22 June to 2 October 1941 saw the German war machine advance to the gates of Leningrad in the north and to the Sea of Azov in the south. Only the onset of the autumn rains, which turned the battlefield into a quagmire, combined with general German exhaustion after more than four months of solid fighting, forced a temporary halt.**

Left: **SS pioneers engaged in the construction of a bridge over one of the many rivers that severely hampered the eastward advance of German forces in the Soviet Union. On the bank above them an SS soldier stands guard alongside a 2cm antiaircraft gun, although the staggering losses inflicted on the Red Air Force by the Luftwaffe during August and September ensured that there would be little chance of sudden air strikes against ground targets such as this.**

Above: **Troops of the 'Reich' Division pass by PzKpfw IIIs of Guderian's Second Panzer Group, which, along with Hoth's Third Panzer Group, formed the striking edge of Army Group Center. The 'Reich' Division was heavily engaged in the great encirclement battles around Minsk and Smolensk. They included an encounter on the old Napoleonic battlefield of Borodino on 15 October, during which divisional commander Gruppenführer Paul Hausser was severely wounded, losing his sight in one eye.**

Left: **The onset of winter during the middle of November 1941 caught the Germans woefully unprepared; characteristically Hitler had gambled on the war being over before the winter set in. Although large numbers of troops had only their summer uniforms, others were better equipped, particularly in the northern regions where the possibility of cold weather had been taken more seriously. Here, SS troops – kitted-out with rudimentary camouflage smocks and snowshoes – drag a machine gun through the snow in January 1942.**

Above: **The height of misery – a young SS trooper finds that greatcoats and scarfs are not enough to withstand temperatures that dropped to minus 40 degrees centigrade.**

Left: **In marked contrast to the photograph above, these SS soldiers are well-prepared for the Russian winter and are thus able to fight effectively. The Soviet counteroffensive launched on 6 December caught the German Army at its lowest ebb, but, although some units fell back in disorder, the troops of the Waffen SS distinguished themselves in the stubborn defensive battles that helped blunt the Soviet attack.**

Above: **Armed with an MG34 general-purpose machine gun, SS troops grimly carry on the battle. The original photograph caption aptly entitled the picture as 'Die weisse Holle' – 'the white hell.'**

Left: **Their (temperate) camouflage smocks being worn over greatcoats, these soldiers warm themselves by a camp fire. In conditions as extreme as these, the qualities of inspired leadership and good morale were vital in maintaining the cohesion and battle-worthiness of SS combat units.**

Right: **The fate of thousands of SS troops during the brutal fighting to stabilize the German line – overrun by a Red Army attack, the men of this SS unit lie where they fell.**

Above: **As the Soviet counteroffensive increased in force, considerable numbers of German troops began to find themselves cut off, isolated from the German frontline in 'pockets,' the most notable being that at Demyansk, which contained six divisions, one of which was 'Totenkopf.' Here, a horse-drawn sledge brings up supplies inside the pocket.**

Below: **The 'Das Reich' commanding officer, Paul Hausser, confers with the CO of the reconnaissance battalion, Fritz Klingenberg, while in the center the divisional chief of staff, Werner Ostendorff, looks at his map.**

Right: **A Junkers Ju 52 makes an air drop to beleaguered 'Totenkopf' soldiers in the Demyansk pocket. Some 500 aircraft were employed in supplying the ground troops during the period from 8 February to 21 April, carrying out anything from 100 to 150 sorties per day. The success of the airlift encouraged both the Luftwaffe and Hitler to overestimate the possibilities of aerial resupply – an error of judgment that helped lead directly to the disaster at Stalingrad.**

Left: **Emphasizing the importance of logistics, Napoleon remarked that an army marched on its stomach, and here we see some of the mass of vehicles required to keep a panzer or motorized division on the move. The rough roads encountered by the Germans in the Soviet Union are clearly visible; German trucks were soon found to be unsuited to traveling great distances in these conditions, and the inevitable breakdowns caused by broken suspensions and transmissions slowed the SS advance eastward.**

Left: **Although it is commonly supposed that the most important attribute of a sniper is his long-range shooting ability, more important still are his skills in field craft and camouflage, for in most cases the sniper's victim is not dispatched by a shot of amazing accuracy at the weapon's maximum range but rather is felled at distances of under 180 meters. This photograph of an SS sniper in southern Russia, taken during the summer offensive of 1942, reveals a somewhat unpractical approach to the problem of concealment; once the sniper had fired his shot he would be overly vulnerable to Soviet counterfire, making withdrawal from any exposed position potentially fatal. Nonetheless, the sniper's camouflage makes for an amusing photograph – probably all that was intended.**

Right: **Another posed photograph, this one showing an SS officer directing a motorcycle dispatch rider during the summer of 1942. The virulence of the Russian mosquito came as yet a further environmental shock to the Germans, and mosquito nets were widely worn in the worst effected areas.**

Left: **An SS cavalry patrol pauses while on a reconnaissance patrol in the Soviet Union. At the outbreak of war in 1939 the German Army maintained its age-old cavalry tradition and throughout the war relied heavily on horse-power for much of its transportation requirements. The SS – despite its 'modern' image – similarly considered that cavalry still had a role to play. In 1940 two mounted regiments were raised, personnel coming from unassigned 'Totenkopf' standarten; a cavalry brigade followed and in September 1942 the 8th SS Kavallerie Division 'Florian Geyer' was authorized.**

Above: **The 'Wiking' Division was at the forefront of the German drive toward the Caucasus Mountains. Snow-capped peaks ahead of them, lead elements of the division halt in a village in the foothills.**

Right: **Commander of the 'Wiking' Division, Obergruppenführer Felix Steiner looks out from a forward observation post during the summer offensive of 1942.**

While the great drama of Stalingrad was being acted out during the winter of 1942-43, SS units had, for the most part, been withdrawn from the combat zones. Better prepared for the cold conditions of this second Russian winter, SS troops in Army Group North found themselves engaged in the standard military activity of 'going out on patrol.' Here, an SS infantryman arms himself for a patrol with a 9mm MP40 sub-machine gun and hand grenades (far left); another trooper makes use of skis for mobility (left); while the snow is carefully examined for signs of enemy activity (right).

Below: **C**lose to the frontline near Leningrad, SS troops take up a position amid the debris of shell casings and ammunition boxes. The coldness of the day is apparent on the faces of the soldiers in the foreground.

Right: **SS artillerymen are brought up to dislodge the Soviet defenders fighting a desperate house-to-house battle in the streets of Kharkov. In the foreground is a infantry gun while behind a Marder self-propelled gun is deployed.**

Below right: **Cumbersome in winter clothing, an SS soldier gives first aid to a wounded comrade. Although the recapture of Kharkov was a signal victory, the Red Army made the Germans pay a high price – a total of 12,000 men dead or wounded.**

Top and above: **An SS Nebelwerfer battery** is unleashed against the center of Kharkov. The 15cm Nebelwerfer 41 was an effective area weapon, consisting of six barrels which could be fired sequentially in 12 seconds, each sending a 70lb high-explosive warhead to a maximum range of 7000 meters. The awesome sight of a Nebelwerfer in action was complemented by its fearful noise – the weapon was known to the British as 'Moaning Minnie.' Area bombardments of urban targets like Kharkov inevitably led to high civilian casualties, although it would seem that this was of little concern to the commanders of the SS Panzer Corps.

Above: **As commander of the SS Panzer Corps, Obergruppenführer Paul Hausser** was responsible for the recapture of Kharkov, a key part of Field Marshal Erich von Manstein's brilliant counterstroke which stabilized the German line following the disaster at Stalingrad. Before joining the SS in 1935, Hausser had already retired from the Army with the rank of acting lieutenant general, and this experience at the higher levels of military command made him a highly respected figure in the SS High Command. Hausser was generally considered to be the most able of the senior SS generals.

Below: **A smiling Obersturmbannführer Kurt Meyer receives the news of the award of Oak Leaves to his Knight's Cross, following the SS Panzer Corps' success at Kharkov.**

Left: **As Soviet resistance begins to crumble in Kharkov, Leibstandarte commanders discuss the next move. Panzergrenadier CO Kurt Meyer (left) makes a point to Sepp Dietrich (center), standing within a SdKfz 251/6, the command version of this famous German halftrack.**

Below right: **While panzergrenadiers perch on the engine deck, tanks of 'Das Reich' move toward the center of Kharkov. The German assault against Kharkov was the first time that the élite Leibstandarte, 'Das Reich' and 'Totenkopf' Divisions had been used together; their success ensured that SS formations would increasingly be deployed at corps level in the future, rather than being grouped with Army divisions on an *ad hoc* basis.**

Left: **Trucks and tanks of the Leibstandarte come to a halt in a side-street following the taking of Kharkov. Just visible on the rear of the tank is the Leibstandarte's divisional insignia: a skeleton key within a shield, in fact a pun on their commander's name, *Dietrich* being the German for a picklock or skeleton key. The leaves under the shield were a later addition following the award of Oak Leaves to Dietrich's Knight's Cross.**

Below: **Battered and burnt-out buildings in the center of Kharkov. Beside being an important communications center and industrial city (T-34s had been built there), Kharkov was a prestige target: before the war the authorities had built up the city as a showcase for communism. Hitler fully realized this and accordingly instructed his generals to spare nothing in the recapture of Kharkov. The prospect of the swastika again flying over the city gave Hitler great satisfaction, and his enthusiasm for the exploits of the Waffen SS gave their panzer divisions a new importance.**

Above: **SS** infantrymen move up to the start line in preparation for the Battle of Kursk. In support are two massive PzKpfw VI Tiger tanks of 'Das Reich' Division, identifiable by the special markings instituted for the battle – an inverted 'T' for Leibstandarte, one with two uprights for 'Das Reich' and three for 'Totenkopf.' After their success at Kharkov, the three SS panzer divisions were kept together in SS Panzer Corps. Deployed on the southern flank of the German line, the SS tanks would help form one of the arms of the pincer movement designed to cut off the Soviet forces in the Kursk salient.

Right: **Even in tanks as large as a Tiger, the crew was subject to the most claustrophobic conditions; the driver's position is shown here with the reinforced glass aperture above the steering wheel.**

Right: **Tanks of 'Das Reich' assemble for the coming battle – the greatest clash of armor in history. Altogether both sides assembled over 6000 tanks and in one particular engagement – the Battle for Prokhorovka – an estimated 2000 armored vehicles took part. To provide protection against hollow-charge antitank projectiles, the PzKpfw IV on the right has been fitted with thin sheets of armor plate around the turret and hull sides known as *Schützen*. A form of spaced armor, *Schützen* was designed to detonate prematurely any incoming hollow-charge projectiles, thereby significantly reducing their ability to penetrate into the tank itself.**

Above right: **Carrying Teller antitank mines, a section of SS panzergrenadiers takes cover beside a knocked-out Soviet T-34.**

Right: **A somewhat unusual photograph taken during a lull in the fighting shows SS officers engaged in a battlefield conference, while behind them is a knocked-out Churchill tank. This Churchill was one of the many armored vehicles sent by the Western Allies (in this case Britain) to help the Soviet Union recover from the drastic losses it sustained during and after Operation Barbarossa. Compared to tanks like the Panther and T-34, however, the Churchill was hopelessly outclassed and, like this example, few survived the rigors of active service.**

Below: **Battle fatigue etched on their faces, these tough-looking veterans from 'Totenkopf' dig into their bread ration. Despite its origins in units used to guard concentration camps, the 3rd SS Panzer Division 'Totenkopf' was an excellent combat formation: Field Marshal von Manstein considered it to be the best SS division that fought under his command.**

Below: **Two SS panzergrenadiers stride through a village which has only just been taken by advancing German forces. Behind them a group of Soviet prisoners awaits transport to the rear and an uncertain fate in captivity. Millions of Soviet soldiers were captured in the great encirclement battles of the Eastern Front, and hundreds of thousands – if not millions – died in German PoW/ concentration camps.**

Above: **The chief medical officer of the Leibstandarte Division, himself wounded in the hand, comforts a more severely wounded comrade.**

Left: **A Soviet soldier talks to his SS interrogator after capture during fighting in the Battle of Kursk. Relatively few Soviet prisoners were taken captive at Kursk, however; the Red Army maintained its front thereby preventing German armored forces from exploiting any breakthrough – as they had done in the great encirclement battles of 1941-42 when Soviet prisoners had been numbered in their hundreds of thousands.**

Below left: **A victim of a Stuka dive-bomber attack this wounded Soviet officer recounts the event to his SS captor, July 1943.**

Right: **A Messerschmitt Bf 110 flies over a detachment of German armor, holding its position in the high grass of the Russian steppes. During the first two years of war on the Eastern Front the Germans were usually able to secure aerial supremacy whenever they wished, but by the summer of 1943 the Red Air Force had recovered from the disasters of 1941 and was successfully competing with the Luftwaffe for control of the skies. The open landscape of the Ukraine made armored vehicles highly vulnerable to aerial attack, as the German panzer units were beginning to discover.**

Below: **Although Kursk represented a major disaster for Germany on the Eastern Front, the SS had fought with their usual determination and won a number of notable local actions. Here, Hauptsturmführer Hans von Charpentier, on horseback, is congratulated by a panzer commander on the recent award of the Knight's Cross. This photograph provides good detail of a Sturmgeschütz (or StuG) III assault gun: the driver's armored vision slit lies directly below the commander's hatch at the bottom of the photograph, while the gun layer's panoramic telescope has been raised so that it can be seen against the vision blocks of the hatch. The StuG III was in many ways a tank on the cheap: a high-velocity 7.5cm gun was mounted directly into the hull of the vehicle, which was based on the PzKpfw III chassis. Despite the lack of a turret the StuG III performed well in a tank-destroyer role and large numbers were deployed on the Eastern Front.**

Left: **A highly decorated Obersturmbannführer of the 'Totenkopf' Division (left) reviews the situation with his staff during fighting in the Ukraine. Beside the awards of the Iron Cross and Knight's Cross, this officer wears the highly prized infantry assault badge.**

Below: **The crew members of a PzKpfw IV pose for the camera on the barrel of their 7.5cm main gun. The partially obscured but recently applied victory rings underline the fact of the hard fighting undertaken by the SS before September 1943, when this picture was taken.**

Right: **Carefully dug in to expose only the minimum amount of gun, this SS 5cm Pak 38 antitank gun is made ready to fire. Firing the tungsten-cored AP40 solid shot, the Pak 38 could penetrate 101mm of armor plate at 740 meters. By way of comparison the T-34/76 had a maximum armor thickness of 60mm.**

Below right: **A cheerful-looking SS trooper prepares to go into action again, his MG42 machine gun resting on his shoulder. During the war the MG42 steadily replaced the older MG34 as the infantryman's standard machine gun: the MG42 was easier to manufacture than the MG34, making good use of steel pressings, and it had a phenomenal rate of fire – 1400 rounds per minute – which was highly disconcerting to an opponent but also potentially wasteful of ammunition.**

Above: An SS soldier prepares to lay a Teller mine, the standard German antitank mine of World War II.

Left: The veteran – a perfect shot of the battle-hardened panzergrenadier beloved of German propaganda.

Right: Not a photograph taken in the tropics, but a picture of two SS soldiers on a water-carrying detail in southern Russia, August 1943. A country of climatic extremes – freezing, snow-bound winters followed by parched, hot summers – the Soviet Union seemed to the Germans to have a weather system working against them. Of these extremes, 'General Winter' was the most dangerous, accounting for thousands of casualties each year.

Above: **A** side view of an **SS StuG III** advancing past infantry entrenchments. The battered state of the StuG III's *Schützen* reveals the rigorous nature of recent fighting.

Left: **The sweet taste of victory – the gun-layer of a Marder III raises his fist in triumph as the panzer's 7.5cm Pak 40 gun knocks out a T-34 on the horizon. The Marder III was a successful example of the German system of utilizing the chassis of an obsolescent tank – in this case the Czech-made PzKpfw 38(t) – as a platform for a new, more powerful gun.**

Below: **Panzergrenadiers leap aboard an SS PzKpfw IV somewhere on the Eastern Front. As there were never enough halftracks to go round, even in the normally well-supplied SS panzer divisions, infantry were forced to use the 'battle taxi' as a means of giving them mobility in the combat area.**

Left: **A Waffen SS police unit rounds up Russian civilians for alleged involvement in partisan activities. The German military authorities, both Army and SS, immediately instigated a brutally repressive regime in any territory under their control. A key element in the German system of control in occupied areas was that of collective responsibility, so that any act of resistance would involve the arbitrary punishment of usually completely innocent civilians. The taking of hostages was standard practice, so that, for example, the killing of any German soldier would be reciprocated with the execution of hostages at a ratio of 10 to the one German.**

Top: **The obscenity of war on the Eastern Front: soldiers from Army and SS units amuse themselves by taking photographs of civilians hanged by the Germans.**

Above: **The lowest of the low – men of an SS Einsatzgruppen (or Action Group), in effect murder squads responsible for the mass shootings of Jews and other peoples on the Nazi death list. Although not part of the Waffen SS, they worked alongside and were given support by the Waffen SS.**

Above: **Oily black smoke pours out of a burning T-34 as SS panzergrenadiers counter a Soviet attempt to cut the road from Kiev to Zhitomir, October-November 1943. The vehicle in the foreground is the well-known German amphibious vehicle, the Schwimmwagen; the propeller unit is positioned at the rear of the car and would be lowered as the vehicle moved into water.**

Left: **An SS infantryman, wearing the winter-issue parka, encourages the men under his command, while in the distance Soviet tanks go up in flames.**

Above right: **The German failure at Kursk in July 1943 was one of the turning points of the war in the East, for from then on the strategic initiative passed over to the Red Army. Consequently the Germans were forced onto the defensive, and the élite panzer divisions acquired the new role of a 'fire brigade,' being rushed from one crisis zone to another, their function being to prevent a Soviet spearhead attack developing into a full-scale breakthrough. Here, SS panzergrenadiers return to base after successfully repelling a Soviet attack against the Kiev-Zhitomir road.**

Right: **Commander of the 'Wiking' Division, Brigadeführer Herbert Gille (right), visits a field hospital to present the Knight's Cross to one of his battalion commanders, Obersturmführer Hans Drexel (lying on camp bed), 14 October 1943.**

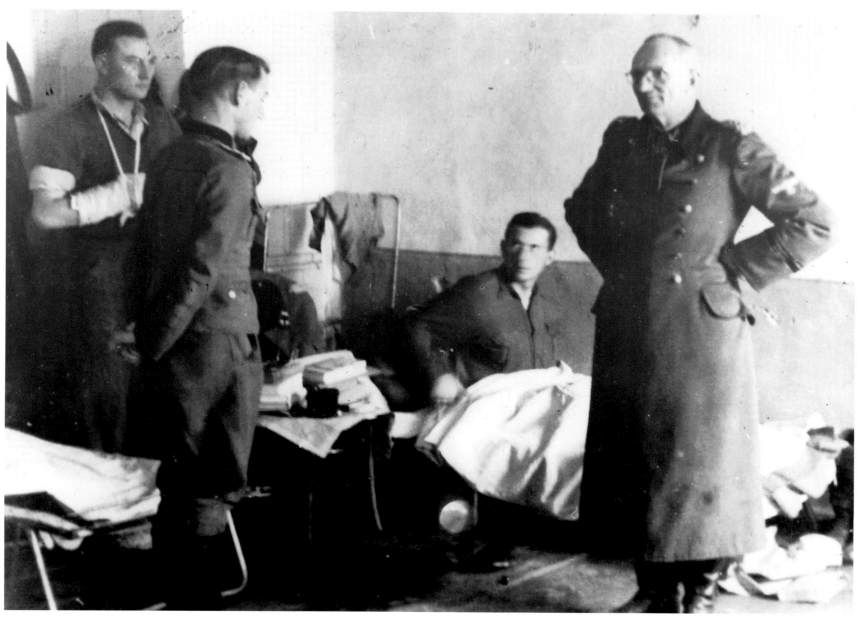

Left: **A photograph taken at an awards ceremony for men of the 2nd SS Panzer Division 'Das Reich' under the command of Gruppenführer Krüger, December 1943. Krüger is seen here talking to a Hauptscharführer of the panzer regiment – wounded in a recent engagement.**

Above: **Leibstandarte soldiers celebrate New Year's Eve 1943 in forward positions near the much fought-over city of Zhitomir. No doubt they are hoping for a more successful 1944 to compensate for the disasters of the former year – a wish that would not be granted.**

Right: **The ample fleece linings of these SS troopers' parkas can be clearly seen: the hoods were made extra large to accommodate a steel helmet.**

Right: **A Hummel self-propelled gun of the 9th SS Panzer Division 'Hohenstaufen' advances across snowy terrain. An effective combination of a 15cm FH18 field howitzer mounted on a hybrid PzKpfw III/IV vehicle, the Hummel formed the mobile element of the panzer division's heavy artillery. The gun was capable of firing a 43.5kg shell to a maximum range of 13,250 meters.**

Left: **Astride their motorcycles, these SS troops enjoy the luxury of hot food, on what, from the evidence of their steaming mess tins, is a typically cold winter's day in the Ukraine, December 1943. The soldier on the right carries a pocket flashlight attached to his chest.**

Above: **As snow begins to fall, a column of SS vehicles pauses on its slow retreat westward across the Soviet Union. Among this disparate collection of vehicles are the Schwimmwagen on the right (widely used on the Eastern Front, where many models were fitted with a tank of special fuel for starting in cold conditions) and a halftrack mounting a 5cm Pak 38 antitank gun, providing the column with a means of defense against Soviet T-34 tanks.**

Below: **The greatest tank ace of the war, Untersturmführer Michael Wittman (left) stands with his crew in front of their winter-camouflaged PzKpfw VI Tiger tank. Wittman served his apprenticeship as a tank-destroyer on StuG IIIs, before being assigned to the Leibstandarte's newly commissioned Tigers early in 1943. Incredibly, within a year, Wittman had increased his score of Soviet tank kills to no less than 117!**

Above: **Operating from a carefully concealed position within a forest in the Baltic region, Polizei troops prepare to fire a 5cm Pak 38 antitank gun. In contrast to the youthful soldiers of the SS panzer divisions, the relatively advanced age of these Pak gunners is evident. As the war progressed, increasing numbers of policemen from 'on the beat' were drafted into SS field units.**

Left: **Still wearing his winter camouflage overalls in March 1944, an SS cavalryman examines the hoof of one of his charges. In the latter stages of the war, while the Army was disbanding cavalry units the SS was increasing them.**

Right: **In the Soviet winter offensive of 1943-44, the 'Wiking' Division was encircled with other German troops in the Korsun-Cherkassy pocket. As the encirclement began to tighten, 'Wiking' instigated a breakout to prevent another 'Stalingrad.' Suffering heavy casualties, the SS troops managed to carve a passage through Soviet lines to safety. Here, CO of a panzergrenadier battalion, Sturmbannführer Hans Dorr (right), discusses the tactical situation with another 'Wiking' officer.**

Far right: **Gruppenführer Wilhelm Bittrich – commander of the 'Hohenstaufen' Division – issues an order to a runner during the successful attempt to rescue the German units trapped in the Kamenets-Podolsky pocket.**

Left: **Obersturmbannführer Max Schäfer inspects damage done to a StuG III self-propelled gun after the spring battles of 1944. Schäfer commanded the engineer battalion in the 'Wiking' Division, and during this period he and his fellow officers were desperately trying to rebuild the shattered division in readiness for the forthcoming Soviet summer offensive.**

Below: **An SS panzergrenadier, his clothing torn but prepared for action.**

Left: **The virtual collapse of Army Group Center during July and August allowed the Red Army to capture large numbers of prisoners, this batch including men from the SS, Army and Air Force.**

Right: **Panzer commander Sturmbannführer Meyerdress confers with an SS officer while on an inspection tour of battalion defenses. Behind the two men is the hulk of a knocked-out Soviet T-34 tank.**

Above: **An Untersturmführer of the 'Totenkopf' Division discusses an order with an Oberleutnant from an Army infantry regiment, September 1944. Paired with 'Wiking' the 'Totenkopf' Division played an important part in reforming the line and holding the Red Army in Poland.**

Below: **'Totenkopf' soldiers rest in a hastily made slit-trench, Eastern Front, 1944.**

Above: **Two SS** cavalrymen engage in conversation during a break in the fighting in Hungary. The trooper on the right is armed with the MP43/StG44 assault rifle. The MP43 used the lower-powered *kurz* cartridge which allowed a fully automatic fire capability within a lightweight weapon. Making use of steel pressings in its manufacture the MP43 was a highly influential rifle, much copied after the war in such designs as the Soviet AK-47.

Left: Adopting a philosophical attitude toward the situation, this **SS** soldier draws on his pipe while awaiting the resumption of a Soviet attack.

Top: **As a Soviet tank goes up in flames behind them, the men of an SS tank-killer team allow themselves some much-needed refreshment. The soldier on the left wears a tank-destroyer badge on his upper right arm, which denotes that he has single-handedly knocked out a tank in close combat.**

Right: **Warsaw burns, 15 August 1944.** As the German armies fell back in disorder into eastern Poland in July 1944, the Polish resistance launched their own uprising in Warsaw itself. On 1 August over 40,000 people of the Polish Home Army rose in revolt, securing key objectives in the city. The SS, under the command of the antipartisan warfare specialist Obergruppenführer Erich von dem Bach-Zelewski, were assigned the responsibility for crushing the Poles, which they did with a barbarity extreme even by their own standards. The Poles had hoped for Soviet aid but this did not come until too late, the Red Army exhausted and regrouping after the previous offensive – although another view suggests that Stalin was only too keen to have the London-based Polish resistance destroy itself prior to a Soviet occupation.

Left: **Oskar Dirlewanger** – convicted child molester, mass murderer and highly decorated **Oberführer**. A protégé of **SS** recruitment svengali, **Gottlob Berger**, **Dirlewanger** formed a special **SS** unit from various groups of – for the most part – convicted criminals: concentration camp inmates, poachers, **Waffen SS** men on probation and cashiered officers from the armed forces. **SS Sonderkommando Dirlewanger** served behind the lines on the Eastern Front, becoming notorious for committing atrocities. During the Warsaw uprising **Dirlewanger** exhorted his troops to commit the most barbarous acts, and complaints leveled against him by the German Army charged him with encouraging looting and even shooting his own men for a bigger share of the loot. **Dirlewanger's** unit acquired brigade status and eventually became one of the last (completely understrength) **SS** divisions – the **36th Waffen Grenadier Division der SS.**

Right: **All hope lost, the Polish commander, General Bor-Komorowski** surrenders to **Bach-Zelewski.** At the end of the war **Bach-Zelewski** immediately began to cooperate with the Allies and became a key prosecution witness at the Nuremberg Trials. For his 'services' to justice **Bach-Zelewski** managed to escape the hangman's noose and received only a suspended sentence.

Left: **Polish civilians are led away as SS** troops prepare to move in. Despite their isolation and shortage of supplies the Poles held their ground remarkably well. Eventually, however, material forces asserted themselves: the **SS** split the defenders into three pockets which, with artillery, rockets and dive-bombers, they then systematically reduced to rubble. Toward the end of September, the Red Army established a link with the beleaguered Poles, but it was too late and on 3 October the remnants of the Polish Home Army surrendered.

Foreign Vo

lunteers

Perhaps the most extraordinary feature of the whole phenomenon of the SS was the transformation of this most German of institutions into a multinational and ultimately multiracial organization. By the end of 1944 the Waffen SS had swollen to a peak figure of around 900,000 men, of whom a half were non-German nationals. In the postwar period many SS apologists described the Waffen SS as a multinational 'pan-European' army specifically raised to fight the communist Soviet Union; in other words the SS assuming the role of an early forerunner of Nato. These clumsy attempts to rehabilitate the SS remain far from the truth, however. The use of foreign personnel was simply a means of helping solve Germany's chronic manpower shortage, so that talk of a 'crusade against Bolshevism' was little more than an eloquent expression coined by SS recruitment officers.

The reasons for the success (and failure) of the various SS recruitment programs (specifically tailored for each nationality) varied enormously, depending on the country's military tradition, its attitude toward Germany, and how well or badly the war was going. At the level of the individual's personal motivation, some SS recruits may have been political idealists violently opposed to communism but these men were very much a minority, most joining – in the West, at least – for other reasons: social 'inadequates' seeking an institutional haven; young men drawn to the glamor of a crack military unit; petty criminals evading justice; desperate individuals transferring from the slavery of Reich labor service; and, during the latter part of the war, collaborators fleeing from retribution in their own countries. Despite the involvement of individuals from almost every country in Europe (including a very small British contingent) foreign troops in the Waffen SS fell into two broad categories, those from Western Europe and Scandinavia and those from Eastern Europe and the Balkans.

According to the perverted nonsense of Nazi Germany's racial theories, the peoples of Scandinavia and the Low Countries were closest to the German Aryan ideal and as such they would be acceptable for recruitment to the Waffen SS. Of the other Western nations, such as France, the latin influence had contaminated their Frankish inheritance but given the constant need for more SS troops, carefully screened Frenchmen need not subvert Himmler's ideals. Altogether, approximately 125,000 'Westerners' served in the SS during the war, of whom about half joined while the war was going in Germany's favor, while the remainder joined during the final stages of the war (in this case, collaborators and Nazi sympathizers). The national breakdown of the 125,000 reflected the broad levels of national sympathy for the Nazis (except for France where right-wingers often joined other specifically French institutions): 50,000 Dutch; 40,000 Belgians (split evenly between Flemings and Walloons); 20,000 French; 6000 Danes; 6000 Norwegians; and around 1200 men from Switzerland, Sweden and Luxembourg. In addition, there were a few oddities which included the 'Legion Indien' – a motley collection of Indian PoWs who never fired a shot in anger – and the 58-strong 'Britische Freikorps' which again was drawn from disaffected individuals in British PoW camps and was of propaganda value only.

The first unit of foreign volunteers to be raised was Standarte 'Nordland' (from Norwegians and Danes) followed by Standarte 'Westland' (Dutch and Flemish) which, with the addition of the native-German SS-VT Standarte 'Germania,' became SS Division 'Wiking' in December 1940. The main impetus to the employment of foreign troops by the Germans came, of course, with the invasion of the Soviet Union in July 1941. In order to make effective use of these foreigners the Germans reluctantly accepted the fact that they would have to co-operate with the pro-German organizations in each country, and that these units would have their own national character. The idea of these national legions was extended from the 'Germanic' countries, like Holland or Norway, to those ideologically sympathetic to Germany, like Croatia. The SS naturally took over the running of the 'Germanic' legions but at this stage of the war Himmler was not prepared to accept 'racially dubious' units from Eastern Europe and so these were assigned to the Army.

The troops in the SS-run legions were distinguished from those in the exclusively German SS formations, by their oath, committing them solely to the war against communism, and by a categorization which implied that they were 'attached to' rather than a 'part of' the Waffen SS. Designated by the new title of 'Freiwilligen' (free will or volunteer) the first of these units was Standarte 'Nordwest,' made up of recruits from Holland and Flanders which subsequently became two separate formations, 'Niederlande' and 'Flandern.' During 1941 they were joined by 'Danemark' and 'Norwegen.'

The recruitment program ran into difficulties, however, when the volunteers found that promises made when they were signing-up were discounted once they had arrived at the training camps. On top of this language barriers between staff and recruits caused friction, and it soon became apparent that the German instructors had little regard for their multinational trainees. Morale in the legions was poor, particularly in 'Flandern' which, after a severe mauling in the Soviet counterattack of early 1942, was eventually disbanded. The other three legions were reinforced and, grouped together at the end of 1942, they were accorded divisional status as 11th SS Freiwilligen Panzergrenadier Division 'Nordland.' The increase in size was paralleled by improvements in training procedure which in turn helped lead to an improved battlefield performance – if not quite of the standard of 5th SS Panzer Division 'Wiking', 'Nordland' was a good fighting division.

Right: **Hitler congratulates Sturmbannführer Léon Dégrelle at an awards ceremony with Felix Steiner (center) looking on. Leader of the Belgian fascist movement, Dégrelle offered his services to the Nazis after the fall of Belgium in 1940 and raised the Wallonische Legion to fight on the Eastern Front. The Legion was under German Army control until 1943 when it passed over to the SS, who renamed the force SS Sturmbrigade 'Wallonien' and subsequently uprated it to an under-strength division, the 28th SS Panzergrenadier Division 'Wallonien.' Although the division was destroyed in the final battles of 1945, Dégrelle slipped out of the country to find a safe haven in Franco's Spain.**

Below: **Soldiers of the SS contingent from Denmark prepare for renewed close-quarters fighting in a deep if hastily dug trench, somewhere on the Eastern Front.**

Toward the end of 1943, 'Nordland' became a German-Scandinavian formation with the removal of the Dutch contingent which was expanded into an independent brigade and then a division, 23rd SS Freiwilligen Panzergrenadier Division 'Nederland.' Grouped together with 'Nordland' the Dutch division fought in the defense of the Baltic cities before being destroyed in the final Battle for Berlin in 1945. Other Western SS formations of note included the 28th SS Panzergrenadier Division 'Wallonien' – transferred from the Army in 1943 as a brigade, it fought with distinction as an understrength division under the command of the Belgian fascist leader Léon Degrelle – and the 33rd Waffen Grenadier Division der SS 'Charlemagne' (franz. Nr. 1) – a French unit of only regimental strength (again transferred from the German Army) but one of the most redoubtable of the defenders of Berlin.

In spite of the good fighting reputation gained by the Western volunteers, they were just too few in number to meet SS requirements. Scattered throughout Central and Eastern Europe were large numbers of Volksdeutsche – people of German descent – who would be acceptable candidates for membership of the SS. In just three countries, Rumania, Hungary and Yugoslavia, it was estimated that there were some 1.5 million Volksdeutsche; clearly this was a rich source of potential recruitment, and by the end of 1943 about a quarter of all Waffen SS personnel were Volksdeutsche.

Recruitment of Rumanian Volksdeutsche began as early as the spring of 1940, but a sudden influx of volunteers from Yugoslavia after the invasion of April 1941 led Berger to suggest to Himmler the formation of an entire division of Yugoslav Volksdeutsche. The need for troops to combat the developing Yugoslav resistance movement was pressing and so on 1 March 1942 the 7th SS Freiwilligen Gebirgs Division 'Prinz Eugen' was authorized, a mountain division designed for antipartisan warfare. Berger and his department had, however, miscalculated the level of support for the new division, but rather than admit defeat Berger used intimidation tactics to encourage the Volksdeutsche to 'volunteer.' Faced with the threat of having their houses destroyed, Yugoslavia's ethnic Germans answered the Reich's summons to join up. Such gangster methods were only a temporary phase as steps were made to introduce formal conscription later in the year. The movement toward conscription marked a general trend; the SS was steadily losing its volunteer approach in the face of the war's insatiable demand for manpower.

Below: **In this French recruiting poster, serried ranks of lantern-jawed SS troops march ever eastward as part of the 'Crusade against Bolshevism.' While many Frenchmen were ready to come to some form of acceptance of the German occupying forces, only a committed few were prepared to join the SS.**

Above: **The Brigadeführer of the 23rd Waffen Gebirgs Division der SS 'Kama' (Kroat Nr 2) climbs aboard a Schwimmwagen amphibious vehicle. The photograph was taken on the roadside by a town in Yugoslavia, the area of operation for this poor-quality and short-lived formation.**

Through intimidation and conscription an impressive numerical level of recruitment was maintained, although this system had one major drawback, namely the poor quality of the personnel sent to the Waffen SS training centers. In the case of the large contingent dispatched from Hungary during 1942, for example, many were totally unfit for military service, even to the point that individuals had to be discharged suffering from complaints as serious as epilepsy and advanced tuberculosis. While such extreme cases could be weeded out, the general level remained chronically poor and consequently the Balkan Volksdeutsche units were second rate.

Yugoslavia, with its mountains and poor road and rail communications, made ideal country for guerrilla warfare and the fact that this newly created state consisted of half-a-dozen mutually antagonistic national-racial-religious groupings gave the ensuing war an especially barbaric character. The Germans were adept in exploiting Yugoslavia's sub-national differences, carving up the country in the process. Slovenia was divided between Italy and Germany, and Italy, Hungary, Rumania and Bulgaria all annexed strips of the country near to their own borders; while Germany set up the puppet state of Croatia – in effect reducing Yugoslavia to a diminished Serbia.

Two resistance movements were not long in emerging, in spite of Germany's divide-and-rule policies. The first was the Chetniks (or Cetniks), led by a monarchist ex-Army officer Colonel Draza Mihailovich; the second, a communist partisan movement under the command of Josip Broz, or Tito as he was better known. The two groups found it impossible to work together and eventually open warfare broke out between them. Tito's partisans were better led and organized, while demoralized and defeated, the Chetniks eventually dropped out of resistance to the Axis forces, eventually reaching the point of actively collaborating with the Germans in an effort to oust Tito. Although the Germans, and their various Balkan allies made strenuous and repeated efforts to destroy the partisan movement they never succeeded, despite coming close to capturing Tito on a number of occasions.

The Volksdeutsche recruitment program was an SS contribution to the war against Tito, and divisions like 'Prinz Eugen' and 'Florian Geyer' were regularly employed in antipartisan sweeps. In contrast to the fighting reputation gained by the 'classic' Waffen SS field divisions, the SS antipartisan units earned for themselves a different reputation, as specialists in perpetrating massacres against the civilian population and other similarly soft targets.

The unique nature of the racial-religious situation in Yugoslavia gave rise to one of the most bizarre of the SS's unconventional formations: the 13th Waffen Gebirgs Division der SS 'Handschar' (kroat. Nr.1). Recruited from Moslems in Croatia in August 1943, it was specifically raised for antipartisan duties; Croatian Moslems had a long-standing hatred for the Serbs and the 'Handschar' Division gained a swift notoriety for the number of atrocities it committed. But as a formation capable of taking on the partisans it proved a dismal failure, and was belatedly disbanded in November 1944 in order to free its German officers and NCOs to fight elsewhere.

The initial interest in employing Moslems for antipartisan duties led to the formation of two further 'divisions': the 21st Waffen Gebirgs Division der SS 'Skanderbeg' (alban. Nr.1) and the 23rd Waffen Gebirgs Division der SS 'Kama' (kroat Nr.2). Both formations never achieved the numerical strength of divisions and were as ineffective as the 'Handschar' in combatting partisans. 'Skanderbeg' was recruited from Albanian Moslems and disbanded after a few months of existence toward the end of 1944, and 'Kama,' originating in Croatia, was similarly disbanded and its numerical designation reassigned to the SS Freiwilligen Panzergrenadier Division 'Nederland.' In short, the SS policy of recruiting Moslems had been a disaster. The very fact that the partisans were able to operate so successfully in the Balkans throughout the war was a testimony to the German inability to exploit minority groups on an effective, long-term basis – in marked contrast to the British, for example, who had great success in this area.

In the Soviet Union, the Germans made somewhat better use of local groups, opposed either to Stalin's government or to the racially dominant 'Muscovite' Russians, and these provided the troops for antipartisan operations. The terrain in the Soviet Union was rarely as favorable for partisan operations as that found in Yugoslavia but the sheer cruelty of the German occupation fanned a vigorous resistance movement into life. Consequently, there were two wars operating simultaneously on the Eastern Front: the conventional war between the two main combatant nations and an equally deadly conflict waged behind the lines.

Until the last two years of the war, when Germany's chronic manpower shortage assumed acute proportions, Himmler had fought to preserve a basic level of racial exclusiveness among the SS. In contrast to this, the German Army had never been burdened by such scruples and, as previously mentioned, had assumed responsibility for the organization of the non-Germanic volunteer groups. The vast majority of these came from within the Soviet Union, from the many non-Russian peoples who had suffered particular hardships during the 1920s and 1930s at the hands of Stalin's brutal Moscow-centered dictatorship.

As the Germans drove deep into the Soviet Union in 1941 they were greeted by large sections of the population as liberators who would free them from the Stalinist yoke. This goodwill could have been turned to great advantage by the Germans, but the Nazis' savage policies alienated many of these potential allies. And yet despite the killings, the deportations and the imposition of a brutal military occupation, the Germans had little difficulty in finding volunteers to act as auxiliaries and behind-the-lines security troops. The most enthusiastic of these were the non-Slavic peoples on the periphery of the Soviet Union: the Balts, Caucasians, Georgians, Turkomens and Cossacks. As the war progressed they were joined by Ukrainians and even Russians, and toward the end it was estimated that as many as a million citizens from the Soviet Union had taken up arms against their communist government.

The erosion of SS racial principles – at least in terms of its recruitment policies – had begun to take effect in earnest with the widespread acceptance of Volksdeutsche. Undoubtedly some of these people prided themselves on their German background and were German in all but nationality, but many more possessed only the most tenuous blood ties with the Reich, so that, for example, a conscripted Volksdeutsche recruit might possess only a Germanic family name, dating back to an ancestor of two or more centuries ago, and so would be unable to speak German or have much affinity with his supposed national heritage. Consequently, it was not such an enormous step from recruiting men who were to most intents Hungarians, Rumanians, Croats and Serbs to Estonians and Latvians, and then to Ukrainians and even Russians.

On 28 April 1943, Ukrainians answered the call for volunteers to form a new SS division in their thousands (almost 100,000 of whom 30,000 were accepted) and by the end of July the 14th Waffen Grenadier Division der SS (galiz. Nr.1) was in being. Over the succeeding months the division was slowly brought to a state of combat readiness. In May 1944 it left for the front but the Ukrainian Division's life would be a short one: in the great Soviet summer offensive of 1944 it was trapped in the Brody-Tarnow pocket and in the ensuing struggle to break out suffered almost 80 percent casualties. Although the 3000 survivors were sent to Slovakia to recover and refit, the division never fought again. Two further Russian-Ukrainian units were raised, and despite their designations were never more than regimental size: the 29th Waffen Grenadier Division der SS (russ. Nr.1) and the 30th Waffen Grenadier Division der SS (russ. Nr.2). Organized out of a nucleus of former security battalions these two 'divisions' were never effective combat units; subsequently they were transferred to the Russian Liberation Army of the pro-Nazi General Vlasov.

In the extraordinary administrative confusion that attended upon the final months of the Third Reich, the Army 'gave' the SS its remaining Soviet acquisitions. These included the exotically named Ostturkischer Waffenverband der SS and the Kaukasischer Waffenverband der SS – from the Soviet Union's southern republics – and a cossack cavalry division. The cossacks had made a fatal commitment to the German side; now that the tide of war had turned against them the cossacks fled westward in an attempt to escape otherwise inevitable Soviet retribution. They were joined by other cossack units, which were organized into a second cavalry division, the two formations being combined into the XVth (SS) Kosaken Kavallerie Korps.

Above: **A Soviet PPSh 41 sub-machine gun slung around his neck, an SS officer briefs his men – a special antipartisan unit raised from Moslems in the Soviet Union – during the suppression of the Warsaw Uprising, 13-14 August 1944.**

Above right: **Cossacks under SS control charge at full tilt, visible evidence of the large numbers of cavalry which operated on the Eastern Front in World War II.**

Left: **Astride their hardy mounts, cossack cavalrymen pause in a Balkan town during their westward retreat from the Soviet Union.**

The cossacks brief period under SS control saw them fighting against Tito's partisans in Yugoslavia, although by 1945 the partisans were not much inconvenienced by these latecomers to mountain guerrilla warfare. On the collapse of their sector of the Eastern Front in April 1945, the cossacks retreated into Austria to surrender to the British rather than face the Red Army. The unfortunate cossacks were politically outmaneuvered, however, and a previous treaty agreement led to their return to Soviet jurisdiction. The cossack leaders were executed while the remainder disappeared inside the Soviet labor camp system.

The three Baltic states of Estonia, Latvia and Lithuania had been swallowed up by the Soviet Union in 1940, and as there was little love between them and their Russian overlords, the former Baltic republics made fertile recruiting grounds for the SS. The German Army had been the first to employ Baltic troops for local defense duties, but following their handover to the Waffen SS in 1943 they were reorganized on divisional lines. Because of Himmler's poor opinion of Lithuanians, only the Estonians and Latvians were taken up by the SS. The end result was the formation of three divisions in 1944: the 15th Waffen Grenadier Division der SS (lett. Nr.1), the 19th Waffen Grenadier Division der SS (lett. Nr.2) and the 20th Waffen Grenadier Division der SS (estn. Nr.1). Almost immediately the new Baltic divisions found themselves thrown into the desperate battles in defense of their homelands. The 19th Division was cut off in the Courland enclave until the end of the war; the 15th SS Division was ripped apart in the defense of German Pomerania; while the 20th SS Division retreated back through Silesia to end the war by surrendering in Bohemia.

* * *

The foreign volunteer movement remained central to the development of the Waffen SS, and yet an obvious question arises: Was it worth it? Questions as 'simple' as this are generally hard to quantify with any degree of precision but in this instance some fairly direct answers emerge. In the case of the Western volunteers, the SS was able to tap a useful source of high-grade manpower which otherwise would have been unavailable to the German armed forces. On the battlefield the Westerners fought well, the ultimate criterion for any military organization. The one major criticism to be leveled against the SS, as far as the Westerners were concerned, was the failure of its officer academies, NCO schools and training grounds to readily accommodate themselves to non-German recruits – a weakness in the system that was corrected far too slowly.

As for the Eastern troops, SS policy can only be seen as an almost unmitigated disaster. On the credit side, the wide range of nationalities involved had some propaganda value in suggesting that the German invasion of the Soviet Union was a 'European' movement intended to rid the world of communism. On the military level, the small Finnish detachments were obviously good soldiers but if they had not fought in the SS these troops would have fought just as well in their own national institutions. As for the others, the Baltic divisions lived up to modest expectations but the remainder were poor at best and at worst a complete disgrace – in fact, quite literally worse than useless. In 1941 and even perhaps in 1942 the whole scheme could have been excused for its propaganda potential, but as the material and manpower shortage began to bite in 1943, it siphoned off trained officers and NCOs desperately needed elsewhere, and in the same way absorbed essential stocks of war munitions.

As in all large, unregulated organizations, 'empire building' became the means of furthering a leader's power within the higher echelons of the hierachy. The creation of so many new SS 'divisions' from 1943 onward undoubtedly increased Himmler's status vis-a-vis the other top Nazis such as Goebbels and Göring. Thus Himmler and his senior SS officers compromised the military efficiency of the SS in favor of short-term political gain. And yet such monumental moral cynicism was one of the building blocks of the Nazi system – and, of course, one of the reasons for its eventual downfall.

Left: **A 7.92mm MG34 machine gun of the 'Wiking' Division is set up in the sustained-fire role against Soviet positions during fighting in southern Russia in 1941. While the 'Number 1' looks through the telescopic sight to ascertain the effectiveness of his shooting, the 'Number 2' fits another belt of ammunition into the gun.**

Right: **Sturmbannführer Hans Dorr, CO of the Panzergrenadier Standarte 'Germania' from the 'Wiking' Division, inspects a Soviet heavy machine gun after a successful counter attack around Kowel, May 1944.**

Left: **A 2cm Flakvierling 38 of the 'Wiking' Division is mounted on a railroad flat car as protection for the formation's armored vehicles, otherwise highly vulnerable to aerial attack when traveling to the front line on trains. The Flakvierling 38 had a high cyclic rate of fire, a maximum effective ceiling of 2200 meters and could fire a variety of high-explosive and armor-piercing ammunition.**

Right: **A 'Wiking' Panther tank advances with panzergrenadiers at the ready during the division's battle to stabilize the line in the summer of 1944 in Poland.**

Left: **The breakout from the Cherkassy pocket was perhaps the finest achievement of the 5th SS Panzer Division 'Wiking'. Hopelessly outnumbered, the division opened up a lifeline to safety for the other formations in the pocket, suffering enormous casualties as a consequence. Here, a column of weary SS troops struggles through the snow during the breakout attempt.**

Below: **Gruppenführer Herbert Gille replaced Steiner as commander of the 'Wiking' division in 1943 and here he speaks to a wounded soldier after being flown into the Cherkassy pocket to plan the breakout. For his efforts he was awarded Diamonds to his Knight's Cross – the first-ever SS soldier to receive that honor. Trained as an artilleryman, Gille was a worthy successor to Steiner and later went on to command the IVth SS Panzer Corps ('Wiking' and 'Totenkopf' Divisions).**

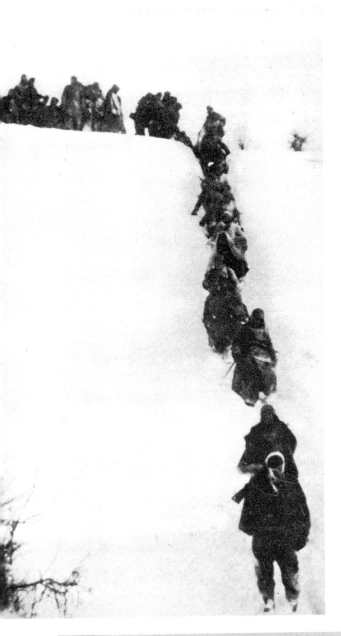

Far left: **Draped with belts of machine gun ammunition, this Norwegian SS volunteer (Freiwillige) pauses for the camera while out on ski patrol.**

Left: **Reichsführer SS Heinrich Himmler discusses the progress of the Norwegian contingent with Stürmbannführer Jonas Lie. At the start of 1943 plans were put into action to form a new 'Germanic' division, consisting of Norwegians and Danes and titled 11th SS Freiwilligen Panzergrenadier Division 'Nordland.' Scandinavian troops already serving in the 'Wiking' Division were the nucleus of the new formation, the remainder being recruited directly in Norway and Denmark.**

Below: **Sturmbannführer Arthur Quist, second-in-command of the Norwegian Freiwilligen. The specific Norwegian insignia on cuffs and collar immediately indicate his nationality.**

Left: **Standing to attention, this color guard of Norwegian volunteers has its standard dedicated on the parade-ground.**

Above left: **A group of battle-weary SS troopers of the 23rd Freiwilligen Panzergrenadier Division 'Nederland' await orders during fighting around Narva on the Eastern Front, March 1944. A companion division to 'Nordland,' 'Nederland' was formed in 1943 with Dutch troops transferred from 'Wiking.' The two new divisions were combined under Felix Steiner's command to form the IIIrd 'Germanische' Panzer Corps which saw heavy fighting in the Baltic area during 1944 and was destroyed in the final battles preceding the fall of Berlin.**

Left: **A military parade including some of the many Dutch troops in the SS who were deployed in the Freiwilligen 'Niederland' before the emergence of the 'Nederland' Division.**

Left: **Arms thrust out in the familiar Hitler salute, young Dutch volunteers leave Holland for the Eastern Front. Typical Nazi graffiti adorn the carriages of the train, but the misplaced idealism of some of these recruits was soon to be shattered by the reality of war against the Red Army.**

Below: **A unit of Dutch SS men is brought to attention before being dispatched to the human meat grinder of the Eastern Front.**

Above: The old Burgundian cross forms the basis of this standard of the Wallonische Legion. Under the leadership of the energetic pro-Nazi Belgian fascist Léon Dégrelle, the Wallonische Legion was quick to establish itself as an important part of the SS in Western Europe.

Left: Cuff-title and sleeve badge of the Freiwilligen Legion Flandern.

Above: **In 1943 the Wallonische Legion was redesignated SS Sturmbrigade 'Wallonien,' and with Dégrelle as CO it was involved in the Cherkassy breakout, supporting the 'Wiking' Division. Inevitably, the brigade suffered heavy casualties but it acquired a new battlefield credibility for its fine combat performance. After being withdrawn to Poland the unit was reformed as a division – 28th SS Panzergrenadier Division 'Wallonien' – which took in recruits from all over Western Europe. To mark the Belgians' achievement at Cherkassy an SS awards ceremony was held in the streets of Brussels: Dietrich (center left) congratulates an SS man while Dégrelle (second from right with field cap) looks on.**

Left: **A railway departure during which volunteers for the Legion Flandern receive bouquets from an enthusiastic crowd in Brussels.**

Above: **After the Fall of France in 1940, many people saw the German swastika and 'Vive La France' as irreconcilable symbols. For the SS, however, they were all part of the 'Crusade Against Bolshevism' and were to be exploited to the full, as in this photograph. The trainload of French Freiwilligen is being sent eastward toward Russia.**

Left: **An NCO dressed in German uniform but with a French national tricolor shield sewn to his right sleeve.**

Above right: **A French SS volunteer (with tricolor on right arm) questions captured French Canadians during the Battle for Caen, Normandy 1944.**

Right: **French recruits to the SS swear a solemn oath to destroy Soviet communism, February 1944. Originally raised by the German Army, pro-German French troops served Germany well, maintaining their good record after being transferred to the SS. In 1943 the French troops were awarded divisional status, replacing an SS cavalry division in the list to become the 33rd Waffen Grenadier Division der SS 'Charlemagne,' although they never exceeded regimental size in numbers.**

Left: **Yugoslav partisans are lined up to be shot by German troops, Smedevevska Palanka, 20 July 1941. The war against the partisans was particularly savage and large-scale atrocities on both sides were commonplace.**

Below: **Men from an SS mountain division help one of their comrades during an exercise in the mountains, somewhere in the Balkans, December 1942.**

Above: **An Obersturmführer gives orders to his men during an antipartisan sweep through the mountains of Bosnia, March 1943. Large numbers of SS troops were semi-permanently deployed in the Balkans for operations of this nature.**

Right: **One of Himmler's most notorious police generals, Heinz Reinefarth, directs a combined SS-Army operation. Reinefarth was an antipartisan warfare specialist and played a leading role in the suppression of the Warsaw Uprising in August 1944. The SS NCO (left) has the Edelweiss badge (the German symbol for mountain troops) on his right sleeve.**

Below: **Gruppenführer Artur Phelps points out a feature of interest to a staff officer of his division, the 7th Freilligen Gebirgs (Mountain) Division 'Prinz Eugen.' The 'Prinz Eugen' insignia can be seen on the collar patch of the officer on the left. Phelps was a former Austrian officer who served as a general in the Rumanian Army before transferring to the Waffen SS in 1941. After command of the 'Prinz Eugen' Division he went on to lead the SS Mountain Corps before his death in Transylvania in October 1944.**

Left: **An Oberscharführer uses an SS motor boat in an antipartisan sweep in the Balkans, 8 June 1943.**

Below, far left: **When the Italians surrendered to the Allies in July 1943, the Germans swiftly and ruthlessly took over their former partner's possessions. Here, SS troops move into the Yugoslav port of Split which had been under Italian control. The armored column is made up of French-built tanks, totally obsolescent in 1943 but used by the Germans away from the main battlefield sectors.**

Below left: **The Germans were not slow to realize the importance of Tito (Joseph Brosz) to the Yugoslav partisan cause and a number of attempts were made to either kill or capture him. The largest of these operations was carried out on 6 June 1944 and involved glider-borne infantry and the SS Parachute Battalion, seen here landing near Tito's headquarters.**

Above: **SS paratroopers occupy a defensive position after their landing, while in the distance plumes of smoke rise up to direct further aerial landings. Despite their efforts, which included the killing of large numbers of partisans and the capture of essential supplies, the SS were unable to take the elusive Tito.**

Below: **A partisan's-eye view of Junkers Ju-52s dropping German paratroopers.**

Left: **Obersturmbannführer Schuemers consults a map while planning an attack on a Greek partisan position in the Thessaly district, December 1943.**

Right: **To the curious surprise of a platoon of German soldiers, a Soviet T-34 advances up the main street of a Balkan town. Captured by the SS, this T-34 is being taken back to Germany for further inspection and evaluation.**

Above: **An SS armored car of Italian origin, complete with death's-head device, is parked alongside a deep hole which marks the place where a major arms cache was hidden by Greek partisans on the slopes of Mount Olympus, December 1943.**

Right: **Commander of the SS Cavalry Division, subsequently the 8th SS Cavalry Division 'Florian Geyer,' Hermann Fegelein (center) holds an impromptu conference with his staff and an Army panzer officer (left). In 1943 Fegelein was transferred to Hitler's headquarters where he became Himmler's liaison officer with the Führer. Despite being married to Eva Braun's sister, he was executed on Hitler's orders at the end of the war after being discovered absent from his post.**

Left: **A Waffen SS recruitment poster from 1941 emphasizes that potential candidates can join up on their seventeenth birthday.**

Right: **A Norwegian poster asking for volunteers for the ski battalion.**

Below: **An interesting Dutch poster making an appeal for men to take part in the struggle against 'Bolshevism.' The pan-European theme became the strongest single element of the SS recruitment message to non-Germans. Hovering in the background of this poster is the face of the famous Boer leader Paul Kruger, something of a hero in the Dutch-speaking world and very acceptable to the Germans as a former enemy of Britain.**

Bli med oss nordover!

Den Norske Skijegerbataljon

ALLES SAL REG KOM

STRIJDT MEE TEGEN HET BOLSJEWISME IN DE WAFFEN SS

WAFFEN SS

Eintritt mit vollendetem 17. Lebensjahr
Kürzere oder längere Dienstzeitverpflichtung

TOONT U EEN WAARACHTIG NEDERLANDER

OP - TEGEN HET BOLSJEWISME !
MELDT U AAN BIJ DE WAFFEN SS
STADHOUDERSLAAN 152 DEN HAAG

Left: **Another Dutch poster using a historical figure as part of its message to gain recruits – Marten Tromp, perhaps the greatest of Holland's many famous admirals and a redoubtable opponent of Britain's Royal Navy.**

Far left: **A fairly typical German recruitment poster, again pointing out that the SS accepted seventeen-year-olds.**

Above: **The Grand Mufti of Jerusalem – an anti-British Arab leader championed by the Germans – inspects rifle accuracy while on a propaganda visit to Moslem troops within the SS.**

Left: **A staff guard of the 13th Waffen-Gebirgs Division der SS 'Handschar' (Kroat Nr 1) stands to attention on the arrival of the Grand Mufti.**

Left: **Men serving in the 23rd Waffen-Gebirgs Division der SS 'Kama' (Kroat Nr 2) were distinctive in their fezzes, but almost totally useless as fighting troops. The 'Kama' Division was disbanded in late 1944, the numerical designation reassigned to SS Freiwilligen Panzergrenadier Division 'Nederland.'**

Above: **Albanians register at the recruitment office of the 21st Waffen-Gebirgs Division der SS 'Skanderbeg' (alban Nr 1), the third of the SS Islamic divisions.**

Above left: **Soldiers of the 'Handschar' Division examine a Nazi-produced pamphlet intended to demonstrate the 'evils' (sic) of Judaism as opposed to the religion of Islam.**

Left: **Having just fired the gun, artillerymen from the 'Handschar' Division sponge out its barrel.**

Above: **Three officers of the 'Kama' Division pose for the camera during preparations for a ceremonial parade in a Yugoslav town.**

Above: **A mosquito net draped over his cap, Colonel General Rendulic listens to a report from an Obersturmführer of the Waffen SS. Rendulic was the Commander in Chief of German forces in Finland and so was responsible for the small contingent of SS troops stationed there.**

Right: **A young SS official war correspondent shows a hunting knife to his opposite number in the Finnish Army. Relations between Finns and Germans were generally good, although Finnish insistence on retaining complete independence of action came as something of a surprise to the German High Command, who were used to dealing with other states as vassals or subordinates.**

Left: **Very well camouflaged with a face net hanging from his helmet, an SS soldier attempts to estimate the range of the Soviet front-line, using a stereoscopic periscope. He is acting as an artillery spotter for an infantry mortar battery; the mortar was an ideal weapon for the rough terrain encountered in Finland's Karelian Forest region.**

Right: **From an observation post deep in the forest, Finnish and SS troops look across toward Soviet front-line positions, November 1941. The Finns were quick to ally themselves with Germany after Operation Barbarossa; for them it was a chance to regain possessions lost in the Winter War of 1939-40.**

Left: **One of the many Soviet citizens who deserted the Soviet cause to fight for the Germans. Originally they were under the direction of the Germany Army, but toward the end of the war they were taken over by the SS. Eventually their numbers were sufficient to form a cavalry corps of two divisions.**

Above left: **Obersturmbannführer Galdins, the commander of a regiment in the 19th Waffen Grenadier Division der SS (lett. Nr 2). His many decorations include both classes of the Iron Cross, the Knight's Cross and the German Cross in Gold (on his right breast pocket).**

Above: **A Cossack cavalryman relaxes beside his faithful steed.**

Top: **A soldier from the 20th Waffen Grenadier Division der SS (estn. Nr 1) guards a 2cm Flak gun which is heavily camouflaged against aerial observation. The Estonian divisional insignia of a sword set within a stylized 'E' can just be discerned on the guard's collar patch.**

War in the

West

When SS units had been 'through the mill' on the Eastern Front, it was common practice to send them to recover in one of the occupied territories of the German Reich. There the exhausted units were refitted and equipped with new vehicles and weapons and, most important of all, a new batch of recruits was dispatched from the divisional depot to be brought up to standard by the remaining veterans. While this process was taking place, the SS unit would act as a force-in-being in whatever country it was stationed. If necessary, a refitting division could be swiftly deployed to act in a variety of new roles, usually to take part in sweeps against local resistance groups. By 1944 increasing numbers of German troops were being stationed in the West in preparation for the forthcoming Allied invasion.

Among these troops were four high-grade Waffen SS divisions: 1st SS Panzer Division Leibstandarte 'Adolf Hitler,' 2nd SS Panzer Division 'Das Reich,' 12th SS Panzer Division 'Hitlerjugend' and the 17th SS Panzergrenadier Division 'Götz von Berlichingen.' This latter division had been formed in France toward the end of 1943 from a mixture of reserve and training units with an injection of Balkan Volksdeutsche to make up the numbers. Both the Leibstandarte and 'Das Reich' had suffered heavily on the Eastern Front: they now faced the task of rebuilding their shattered units with replacements considerably inferior to those they

Right: **The Allied breakout from the Normandy beachhead, August 1944. While the British and Canadian armies pushed southward from Caen, the Americans broke through the Avranches gap and swept around westward, virtually trapping the Germans in the Falaise pocket. By then the hard-pressed SS panzer divisions were too exhausted to hold the Allies back, although they were instrumental in holding open the Falaise gap for a sufficient time to allow thousands of German soldiers to escape the Allied encirclement.**

Below: **A rare moment of quiet for Sepp Dietrich, who at the time of the Normandy landings was commander of the 1st Panzer Corps.**

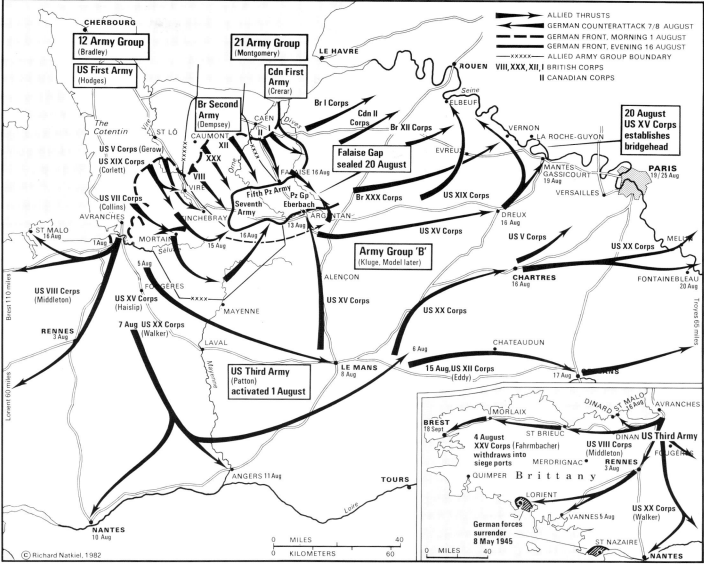

had been used to in the earlier years of the war. Nevertheless they still retained a nucleus of battle-hardened veterans who formed the essential core of each formation.

The 12th SS Panzer Division 'Hitlerjugend' was one of the most successful examples of German utilization of the nation's human assets. In January 1943 the leadership of the Hitler Jugend (Hitler Youth) – very roughly equivalent to the Boy Scout movement – suggested to the SS the formation of a new division to be filled by the older boys of the organization. There was no shortage of Hitler Jugend volunteers imbued from early childhood with Nazi ideals, and of all the SS divisions this was by far the most fanatical: any lack of experience was compensated for with an extraordinary enthusiasm for combat. The leadership of the division was provided by officers and NCOs transferred from the Leibstandarte, thereby grafting experience onto the teenage rankers' enthusiasm. The two divisions remained in close association throughout the war and were combined into the I SS Panzer Corps for the Normandy landings, led by the Leibstandarte's old commander Oberstgruppenführer Sepp Dietrich.

When the Allies came ashore on the morning of 6 June 1944 the SS divisions were scattered across France. 'Hitlerjugend' was stationed nearest the landing site, between the Orne and the Seine, with the Leibstandarte deployed farther to the east. 'Gotz von Berlichingen' was held in the Loire Valley and farther south still was 'Das Reich,' its units situated in and around the small Gascon town of Montauban in south-western France.

The Germans, suffering from an over-complex High Command system, were slow to react but the 'Hitlerjugend' division was the first SS formation to enter the fray with advance units under Kurt 'Panzer' Meyer's command launching an ad hoc counterattack on 7 June. The ferocity of the SS assault came as an unwelcome shock to the Allies but their command of the air prevented the proper deployment of the 'Hitlerjugend' Division whose attack came to an untidy and frustrating halt.

This first attack of Meyer's would set a pattern for the next two months of bloody fighting: the panzer units were the trump card in the German pack but they were virtually impossible to play. Daylight movement by anything other than the smallest unit brought down an immediate aerial attack and, when in range, a devastating pounding from the Allied guns – both sea and shore-based. Adequate fuel supplies for the ever-thirsty panzers were a constant problem too, exacerbated by regular Allied rocket attacks on fuel dumps. Deprived of their mobility the panzer divisions were forced on to the defensive, but only through the adoption of aggressive, offensive action could the Allied invaders be thrown back into the sea.

Together with the Leibstandarte and the 21st Panzer Division, the 'Hitlerjugend' was assigned the task of defending the key positions in and around the city of Caen on the German right flank. They were reinforced from 20 June onward by the arrival of the 9th SS Panzer Division 'Hohenstaufen' and the 10th Panzer Division 'Frundsberg,' following their transfer from Russia to the West. Meanwhile, the two other SS divisions were struggling northward. 'Götz von Berlichingen' arrived at the battle front on 11 June, facing the American sector, its progress constantly hampered by Allied bombing strikes.

On its journey from Montauban 'Das Reich' was subjected to a series of time-consuming ambushes and acts of sabotage by members of the French Resistance. Enraged by these 'bandit' actions the SS troops crushed all signs of resistance, and as the advance slowed down even more they committed two outright atrocities. In the small town of Tulle – scene of a recent Resistance attack – 99 Frenchmen were rounded up as potential Resistance members and hanged from the lampposts on the town's main streets. Farther along the route an SS officer was killed by Resistance men. The town nearest the scene of the killing, Oradour-sur-Glane, was arbitrarily selected for the SS reprisal. The 642 inhabitants – men, women and 207 children – were shot or burned to death and the village systematically destroyed by explosives and fire. (Another theory suggesting a very different reason for the killings has recently been advanced – see Bibliographical Note, page 190.) 'Das Reich' eventually reached its positions north of St Lô by early July: a severe delay at a critical phase of the campaign, but one bought at a high price in innocent French lives.

Throughout June and July 1944 the six SS divisions struggled ceaselessly to contain the Allies in their Normandy beachhead. The Allies advantage of numbers and strength was pitted against the Germans' superior armored vehicles and tactical skill. If the Allies controlled the sky, so the high hedgerows and confined spaces of the Normandy *bocage* country greatly favored the defenders. Masters in the craft of flexible defensive fighting, the SS troops took a heavy toll of Allied armor. Cromwell and Sherman tanks – inadequately armored and woefully undergunned – stood little chance against the high-velocity guns on the German panzers.

The most devastating example of superior German combat performance was illustrated in the engagement at Villers Bocage on 13 June. A column of tanks from the British 7th Armoured Division was spotted advancing out of Villers Bocage by a Tiger tank commanded by Hauptsturmführer Michael Wittman, a veteran of the Eastern Front and a top panzer 'ace.' As the British column halted on the road the lead half-track was blown to smithereens by a perfectly placed shot from Wittman's Tiger tank. The ensuing disaster is

Above: **Wearing Italian camouflage uniform, an officer of the 12th SS Panzer Division 'Hitlerjugend' gives an order to one of his men.**

Right: **Senior officers of the 'Hitlerjugend' Division discuss their increasingly desperate tactical situation. Fritz Witt (center) was the division's CO, Kurt Meyer (left) commanded the 1st Panzergrenadier Regiment and Max Wünsche led the 'Hitlerjugend' tank regiment.**

Left: **Wounded SS soldiers are led away to captivity by Anglo-Canadian troops in the Caen area.**

vividly described in Chester Wilmot's *The Struggle For Europe*: 'Out of the woods to the north lumbered a Tiger tank, which drove on to the road and proceeded right down the line of half-tracks "brewing up" one vehicle after another. Behind them there was some incidental armor – a dozen tanks belonging to Regimental HQ, the artillery observers and a reconnaissance troop. The Tiger destroyed them in quick succession, scorning the fire of one Cromwell, which saw its 75mm shells bounce off the sides of the German tank even at a range of a few yards! Within a matter of minutes the road was an inferno with 25 armored vehicles blazing.'

Extraordinary though Wittman's exploit was, the weight of the Allied *Materialschlacht* remorselessly ground the Germans down. On 31 July the Americans broke out of the beachhead and, sweeping south and then eastward, threatened to encircle the German divisions around Caen. One last attempt was made to restore the situation: an all-out assault on the American supply bottleneck at Avranches, spearheaded by four panzer divisions, including the Leibstandarte and 'Das Reich,' under the command of the veteran SS commander Oberstgruppenführer Paul Hausser. Yet again, Allied ground-attack aircraft stopped the tanks in their tracks; superior artillery and a resolute Anglo-American defense wore down the attackers so that the once superbly equipped SS armored divisions were reduced to ad hoc battle groups.

The German position in Normandy was becoming dangerously untenable: as the

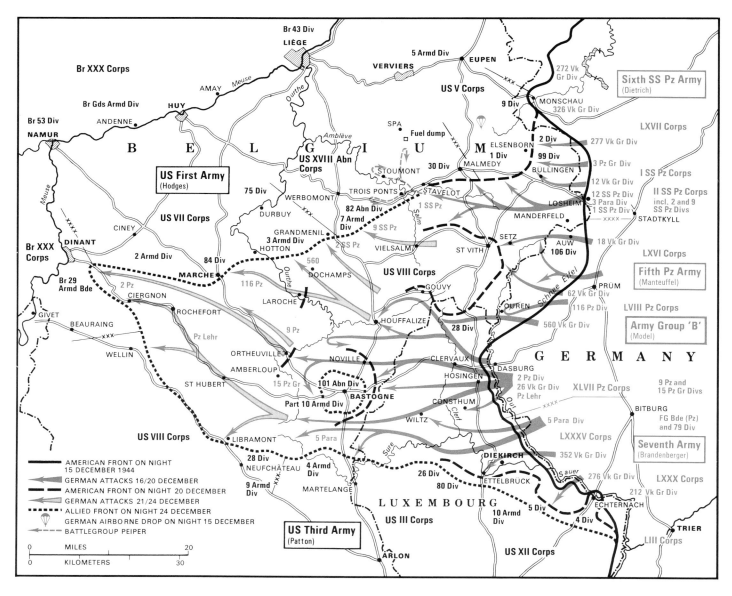

Above left: **The Battle of the Bulge – the German spearhead advance through the Ardennes, December 1944. The offensive was Hitler's last gamble, but in the face of superior Allied material force (especially in the sphere of air power) it was doomed to failure.**

American armored columns under General Patton raced across France, curving round to meet the British advancing south from Caen, the envelopment of the Germans became a growing possibility. By the middle of August a total of 19 German divisions were virtually caught in a pocket with only a small gap between Falaise and Argentan open to safety in the east. As the Allies close in, the remnants of the 'Hitlerjugend' held the gap open around Falaise while 'Das Reich' and 'Hohenstaufen' did the same on the southern lip of the pocket's exit. A complete disaster was averted, largely due to the efforts of the SS and although 50,000 prisoners were taken many more escaped the Allied pincers. Increasingly, while ordinary German soldiers were prepared to surrender to the Allies, it was left to the SS to fight on. Casualties were correspondingly heavy: 'Hitlerjugend' had lost 80 percent of its armored fighting vehicles, 60 percent of its artillery and 80 percent of its personnel, which by September amounted to a mere 600 men.

During the autumn of 1944 the Allied advance across France began to slow down – a consequence of over-extended lines of supply and communication – thereby allowing the battered German armies time to recover and to establish new defensive positions. Toward the end of September the Allies made a last attempt to break through the German line as part of Operation Market Garden, the series of airborne landings that culminated in the daring but ill-fated attempt to secure a bridgehead across the Rhine at Arnhem.

The planners of the British assault on Arnhem unfortunately ignored Resistance reports of the presence of the 9th and 10th SS Panzer Divisions in the area; the SS troops were undergoing a refit after their ordeal in the Normandy battles. Although the British caught the Germans completely by surprise when the first parachute drops were made on 17 September, the SS recovery was typically swift and after a couple of days of hard, close-quarters fighting they regained the initiative. German superiority in overall numbers and in the heavy weapons at their disposal made British defeat inevitable; on 25 September the remnants of 1st Parachute Division retreated back across the Rhine.

A notable feature of the battle was the mutual respect held for the fighting abilities of each side. Certainly, the young veterans of the 'Hohenstaufen' and 'Frundsberg' divisions impressed their British opponents, and their chivalrous regard for the British wounded was a far cry from the murderous behavior of elements of the 'Hitlerjugend' in Normandy, where there had been several instances of Canadian prisoners being killed by their SS captors.

The recovery of the German war machine in the final months of 1944 was sufficient to convince Hitler to launch a major offensive against the Allies in the West. In essence, an

Above: **Overseen by a British soldier, two German prisoners (SS man on right) are instructed to chop firewood within the Oosterbeck perimeter, September 1944. The quick response to the British landings at Arnhem by the two divisions of Obergruppenführer Wilhelm Bittrich's SS Panzer Corps was one of the factors that led to eventual German victory.**

Above right: **Sturmbannführer Otto Skorzeny. After two triumphantly successful missions, rescuing Mussolini and overthrowing the Horthy regime in Hungary, much was expected of Skorzeny in his next operation in support of the Ardennes offensive.**

attempt to repeat the success of the 1940 breakthrough, Hitler's 1944 offensive through the Ardennes was to take the form of a massive armored thrust toward Antwerp, thereby attempting to divide the British from the Americans. As with so many of Hitler's undertakings it was a major gamble, and in retrospect it was obvious that the Germans would have done better to husband their resources in the West in favor of conducting an aggressive defensive campaign against the Red Army in the East.

i   Two panzer armies were assembled to spearhead the assault: the Fifth Panzer Army under General Hasso von Manteuffel and the Sixth SS Panzer Army, the larger of the two forces, which would be commanded by the Führer's old chauffeur and bodyguard, Oberstgruppenführer Sepp Dietrich. The nucleus of the SS force was the 1st, 2nd, 9th and 12th SS Panzer Divisions, which, it was hoped, under the cover of surprise and bad weather (grounding the Allied fighter-bombers), would overrun the light screen of American troops holding the Ardennes.

On 16 December German tanks surged forward across the American lines, advancing deep into enemy territory during the first few days of the offensive. The hills and narrow defiles of the Ardennes naturally favored the defense, however, and to the surprise of the Germans the disparate collection of US units facing them put up a surprisingly effective resistance. Making good use of natural obstacles the Americans refused to be dislodged; by 21 December the German advance was running into trouble with long lines of vehicles strung out in massive traffic jams. The SS units – much to their chagrin – suffered from these hold-ups even more so than the Army and true to form this frustration was eventually to translate itself into the committing of atrocities: this time, the slaughter of American prisoners outside the town of Malmédy.

The reinforced battle group from the Leibstandarte under Obersturmbannführer Joachim Peiper made good progress in a dash to outflank the key position of Liége from the south, but after reaching Stavelot his progress was stopped by the timely arrival of American reinforcements. The improvement of the weather from 24 December onward, combined with the excellent use of reserves by the Anglo-American High Command, ended any hope of German victory. As usual Hitler refused to accept the inevitable and even launched a subsidiary offensive in Alsace, spearheaded by the 17th SS Panzergrenadier Division, but this came to nothing except to swell the German casualty figures to well over 100,000 men. Losses in material were equally serious and included the destruction of over 600 armored fighting vehicles, 13,000 motor vehicles and over 1600 aircraft. As the New Year dawned Hitler's attention began to turn eastward and accordingly the SS divisions were pulled out of line in the West in preparation for their last great battles of the war on the Eastern Front.

Right: **A column of vehicles of the 1st SS Panzer Division Leibstandarte 'Adolf Hitler' pauses on a road leading out of Milan, August-October 1943. The Leibstandarte had been withdrawn from the Battle of Kursk and dispatched to Italy on Hitler's personal orders after the Allied landings in Sicily in July 1943. The division was not deployed in the front line, however, but instead acted to bolster the remains of the Italian fascist state following the overthrow of Mussolini on 25 July. Stationed in northern Italy the Leibstandarte was employed in antipartisan activities which included a particularly brutal massacre of the civilian population of the village of Boves. In November the deteriorating situation in Russia forced the SS division's return to the Eastern Front.**

Above: **Wearing camouflage face veils, Waffen SS troops prepare to fire a mortar on the Italian Front. The weapon in question is a 10cm Nebelwerfer 35; an enlarged version of the 8cm Granatwerfer 34, it was capable of firing high-explosive bombs as well as the smoke rounds it was originally designed for. The Italian campaign was not an important area of Waffen SS participation, with the exception of the 16th SS Panzergrenadier Division 'Reichsführer SS,' elements of which fought at Anzio and in the long defensive withdrawal up the Italian peninsula.**

Below: **Mussolini was arrested by the Italian authorities after his overthrow and held at the Gran Sasso hotel, high in the Abruzzi Mountains. Led by Sturmbannführer Otto Skorzeny, a mixed SS/paratroop force mounted an extraordinarily daring airborne-rescue operation on 12 September 1943 which snatched the dictator away from his captors to the safety of German-occupied Italy. Here, Skorzeny (left) leads Mussolini (center) away from the hotel to the aircraft waiting to fly them away.**

Bottom: **One of the gliders used to fly in Skorzeny's assault group; the dramatic (and dangerous) terrain around Gran Sasso is evident.**

Bottom left: **Skorzeny acknowledges the congratulations of the crowd at a ceremony in the Berliner Sportspalast, 3 October 1943. As leader of the special SS commando unit, Skorzeny subsequently masterminded 'covert' operations in Hungary and the Ardennes.**

Right: **A party of Hitler Youth members gets ready to march out on parade at a summer camp in Berlin before the war. Germany had a long tradition of youth movements and the Nazis were not slow in exploiting these groups to further their own ends. Once the party was in power the various youth movements were brought together in the single entity of the Hitlerjugend (Hitler Youth), which became a fanatical pro-Nazi organization under the leadership of Baldur von Schirach.**

Below: **A bizarre combination of boy scouts, soldier cadets and street-corner informers (denouncing parents for anti-Nazi sentiments was particularly encouraged), the prewar Hitler Youth was essentially an ideological tool for propagating the Nazi message. Once war came, however, and Germany's manpower shortages became increasingly acute, members of the Hitler Youth found their true role as auxiliaries to the war effort, their duties ranging from carrying dispatches to operating searchlights for antiaircraft batteries. The children in this photograph engage in a tug-of-war exercise while dutifully wearing steel helmets and gas masks in preparation for a possible air raid.**

Below: **According to the original caption, this Hitler Youth trumpeter blows reveille at a summer camp in Austria – then part of the German Reich. Significantly, the trumpet banner displays a single SS sigrune: halfway to the fully fledged twin runes of the SS proper.**

Auch Du

Left: **The Italian youth leader 'Undersecretary' Ricci inspects a line-up of Aryan youth while paying a visit to his opposite number, Baldur von Schirach (far left), 2 May 1937. Membership had expanded dramatically during the 1930s, reaching a ceiling of over eight million (including both sexes) in 1938, making the Hitler Youth a not insignificant cog in the Nazi machine.**

Above: **The formation of the 12th SS Panzer Division 'Hitlerjugend' from Hitler Youth volunteers represented the logical conclusion to the Nazi youth program. The core of the division would be provided by the 'class of 1926'; experience came from officers and NCOs transferred from the Leibstandarte 'Adolf Hitler.' This straightforward recruiting poster compares the Hitler Youth boy with the Hitler Youth soldier, the legend translating roughly as 'And you as well.'**

Above: **A collection of senior SS officers observes the 'Hitlerjugend' Division during its 'training-up' period at Beverloo in Holland, summer of 1943. Sepp Dietrich stands foreground center with field glasses, while on the far right is Standartenführer Fritz Witt. Originally, the powerful chief of the SS recruitment office, Gottlob Berger, had pleaded with Himmler for command of the new division but the Reichsführer SS wisely refused the desk-bound warrior's request, turning instead to Witt, the highly experienced commander of the 1st Panzergrenadier Regiment of the Leibstandarte 'Adolf Hitler.'**

Far left: **An NCO of the newly formed 12th SS Panzer Division 'Hitlerjugend' strums a guitar, Western Front 1943-44. A notable feature of the 'Hitlerjugend' uniform was the wearing of leather surplus stock from Germany's U-boat arm.**

Center left: **A good view of SS camouflage as worn by a 'Hitlerjugend' soldier, Holland 1943.**

Left: **A PzKpfw IV of the 'Hitlerjugend' Division negotiates a swing-bridge while on maneuvers in Holland.**

Above: The mangled remains of a PzKpfw VI Tiger I, ripped apart by Allied tactical bombers during the SS attack against US positions around St Lô. To their intense frustration, the veteran SS tankmen found themselves unable to operate effectively, their mobility inhibited by Anglo-American fighter-bombers.

Right: A column of PzKpfw VI Tiger Is of Abteilung 101 moves up toward Normandy shortly after D-Day. Abteilung 101 was the heavy tank battalion assigned to the 1st Panzer Corps, composed of the Leibstandarte and the 'Hitlerjugend' Divisions.

Right: **A motorized column from the 'Hitlerjugend' prepares to engage the enemy; it was the first SS division into action, blocking the Anglo-Canadian advance toward the strategically vital town of Caen during the first couple of days of the Allied invasion.**

Below right: **A French policeman guides an SS unit rushing toward the Invasion Front during the desperate days of June when the success of the Allied landings seemed to hang in the balance.**

Below: **Wittman (left) talks to his crew in a forest clearing in Normandy, June 1944. Although a great tank commander by any standards, Wittman was fortunate in his gunner, Balthazar Woll (second from right with Knight's Cross at neck), who, in an age of simple gun-stabilizing systems, when it was customary to fire an aimed shot while stationary, was able to fire his gun on the move. Wittman's luck was not to last, however, for on 8 August his Tiger tank was surrounded by at least five Allied Sherman tanks: one shot from the Shermans smashed its way through the Tiger's side armor, killing the entire crew.**

Above: **Brigadeführer Fritz Witt (seated in sidecar) is driven on a reconnaissance mission by Standartenführer Kurt Meyer during the early days of the invasion. On 16 June Witt was killed by an explosion from a 15-inch shell fired from an Allied offshore battleship, command of the division passing to the 33-year-old Meyer.**

Right: **Obersturmführer Michael Wittman, the Leibstandarte tank ace, sits on the mantlet of his Tiger tank's 8.8cm KwK 36 main gun. The tank has been coated with Zimmerit paste, a device to prevent the placing of magnetic mines on the tank sides and hull.**

Right: **Wearing the distinctive Italian camouflage uniform which Leibstandarte troops had picked up during their Italian sojourn in 1943, Max Wünsche surveys the tactical situation from the cupola of his PzKpfw V Panther tank. By now Wünsche was in command of the 'Hitlerjugend' panzer regiment, which comprised two battalions of tanks, one of Panthers and the other of PzKpfw IVs.**

Below right: **British prisoners slump on an SS SdKfz 251 halftrack during the fighting in Normandy, July 1944.**

Left: **Draped with ammunition belts, men of the 17th SS Panzergrenadier Division 'Gotz von Berlichingen' line up for inspection, June 1944. This division was raised in France during the summer of 1943, its personnel drawn from a variety of sources, including replacement drafts and rear-echelon troops from existing German SS units, plus a number of Volksdeutsche from the Balkans. 'Gotz von Berlichingen' was heavily engaged in the Normandy battles, fighting alongside the 2nd SS Panzer Division 'Das Reich' in a stubborn but ultimately unsuccessful attempt to prevent the American breakout.**

Below: **Two men of the 'Hitlerjugend' Division man a 7.5cm Pak 40 antitank gun in the bocage country of Normandy. A fearsome weapon, the Pak 40 was by 1944 the standard antitank gun of the SS divisions, and was capable of penetrating 98mm of armor plate at a range of 2000m.**

Above: **The color guard of the Leibstandarte 'Adolf Hitler' leads the funeral procession at the burial of the 'Hitlerjugend' commander, Fritz Witt. Despite the desperate situation facing the SS in Normandy, an officer of Witt's distinction and popularity still received full military honors.**

Above left: **An Unterscharführer of the Leibstandarte in Normandy 1944; the divisional monogram on his shoulder strap is clearly visible in this photograph.**

Left: **A young SS soldier, wounded in the face, surrenders to the Allies during the Normandy campaign, June-July 1944. Although his wound would seem to be a consequence of direct military action, this photograph has been previously captioned as an example of an SS soldier being beaten up by Canadian troops after surrendering. Certainly, relations between the 'Hitlerjugend' and their Canadian opponents in Normandy deteriorated rapidly once the Canadians discovered that the SS had murdered their fellow countrymen when they were behind-the-lines prisoners. At the end of the war, the 'Hitlerjugend's' commander, Kurt Meyer, was found guilty and sentenced to death for these killings. The sentence was commuted to life imprisonment, however, and Meyer was subsequently released in 1955.**

Right: **A wounded SS soldier is helped into a truck during the German retreat from Normandy in August 1944.**

Below: **A once-mighty SS PzKpfw VI Tiger tank of Abteilung 101 lies destroyed in the rubble of Caen, the victim of overwhelming Allied air power.**

Right: **Supported by a StuG III assault gun, troops move through the streets of Arnhem as part of Bittrich's plan to counterattack the British 1st Airborne Division. Although surprised by the initial Allied airborne landings on 17 September 1944, the 9th and 10th SS Panzer Divisions were both swift and resolute in their handling of a difficult tactical situation.**

Far right: **The famous 'Bridge Too Far' – the main Rhine crossing at Arnhem. Visible in this aerial photograph, taken shortly after the battle, are the British positions on both sides of the bridge to the north and the remains of burnt-out vehicles yet to be cleared by the Germans.**

Below: **British prisoners await medical attention from their SS captors. In contrast to so many operations involving the SS, Arnhem was characterized by an observance of the Geneva Convention.**

Right: **As part of a combined SS and Army operation, German troops dig in to prevent the British from breaking out of their main positions around Oosterbeck to the west of Arnhem.**

Far right: **The SS made good use of the nearby assault-gun battalion when the British paratroopers landed at Arnhem; many British accounts refer to the effectiveness of the German StuG IIIs during the house-to-house fighting toward the end of the battle. Here, a German self-propelled gun, obscured by a British parachute, lurks beside a partially destroyed Dutch house.**

Above: **German paratroops hitch a ride on a PzKpfw VI Tiger II attached to the Leibstandarte 'Adolf Hitler' during the early stages of the great German offensive in the Ardennes, December 1944.** Weighing just under 70 metric tonnes, the Tiger II was the armored monster of the World War II battlefield. Its hull armor was up to 150mm thick (providing almost total protection from Allied tank guns) and its main armament consisted of an uprated 8.8cm KwK 43 gun whose armor-piercing capability was superior to that of the Tiger I. The Tiger II's great weakness, however, was that it lacked a suitable powerplant; its 700hp Maybach engine and transmission was not sufficient to drive such weight and the Tiger II was plagued with reliability problems during it short-lived operational life.

Right: **An SS soldier marches past a burning American halftrack on the second day of the Battle of the Bulge, 17 December 1944.**

Left and below: **Stills from a German propaganda film (likewise, photograph opposite page below) showing the opening stages of the German attack. Among the booty captured from the retreating Americans are the rainproof coats worn by the SS troops in these photographs.**

Left: **SS troops from the Leibstandarte pause by a roadside signpost during the Battle of the Bulge. They are riding in a Schwimmwagen, the amphibious version of the Kubelwagen, which was the standard light vehicle of the German armed forces during the war.**

Left: **Smoking captured US cigarettes, these SS troops push forward in an attempt to sustain the early momentum of the German advance. The soldier in the foreground has armed himself with a US MI carbine, a handy gas-operated weapon which was highly popular with German troops able to lay their hands on it. The MI's only disadvantage was its lightweight cartridge which affected its range and overall stopping power.**

Above: **The wreckage of shot-up American vehicles behind them, SS troops run across a road in the Ardennes. The poor weather – snow and low cloud, particularly – was of great advantage to the Germans during the early stages of the offensive; when it improved, however, the SS armored columns became highly vulnerable to Allied fighter-bombers.**

Right: Under the gaze of SS troops, a group of American soldiers marches into captivity. The worried expression on their faces was understandable: the SS already held a reputation for fanaticism and at Malmédy they did murder American prisoners in their charge.

Above right: SS troopers walk past knocked-out American armored cars.

Left: **Soldiers of the US 82nd Airborne Division bring a captured SS trooper back to the Allied lines. The veteran US soldiers of the 82nd were rushed to the Ardennes sector and played an important part in blunting the SS attack.**

Below: **By the end of 1944 the SS were scraping the barrel to find the necessary troops for even their best divisions. These two SS youths were captured by US troops near Bastogne; the disparity between the Americans and the Germans is only too evident in this photograph.**

Right: **The victims of the Malmédy massacre are carefully photographed by US military authorities prior to burial. They were killed by men of Kampfgruppe Peiper, a detachment from the Leibstandarte, during the initial stages of the German attack in the Ardennes.**

Below: **Under the command of Otto Skorzeny, a special unit of English-speaking troops was employed to infiltrate the American front line wearing Allied uniforms. Their role was to perform sabotage and intelligence missions which would hopefully spread confusion in the American rear areas. Once the Americans became aware of their activities, however, they were swiftly rounded up, tried as spies and sentenced to death. These three were the first to be captured and shot by a US firing squad.**

Götterdä
The End o

mmerung:
f the SS

The failure of the German panzer divisions to break through in the Ardennes and the opening of the great Soviet offensive on 12 January 1945 spelled the end of the Nazi regime in Germany. And yet there would be nearly four months of bitter fighting during 1945 before Hitler took his own life in the ruins of Berlin on 30 April. In this final year of the war the Waffen SS was deployed almost entirely on the Eastern Front in what would turn out to be a vain attempt to stem the inexorable progress of the Red Army.

Even as the Soviet High Command began to deploy its vast forces for the invasion of Germany, Hitler's main concern was to safeguard the tenuous hold he still maintained over the Hungarian oilfields. Budapest, scene of a concerted Soviet attack during the winter, had been surrounded and a large German garrison trapped within the city perimeter. Among the encircled divisions were those of the IX SS Corps, comprising the 8th SS Kavallerie Division 'Florian Geyer' and the 22nd Freiwilligen Kavallerie Division der SS 'Maria Theresia.' In an attempt to raise the siege the two elite SS divisions 'Totenkopf' and 'Wiking' were transferred from their key positions on the German-Polish border. A month-long battle failed to relieve the city although the SS troops took a heavy toll of the Soviet besiegers. By early February the situation for the Germans in Budapest was reaching crisis point and despairing of any rescue a breakout was instigated: of an original garrison of 50,000 men a mere 785 soldiers made it back to German lines.

The transfer of the Sixth SS Panzer Army from the West to the Hungarian Front had been constantly delayed and so it could take no part in preventing the Red Army from capturing Budapest on 13 February. Five days later, however, the 'Hitlerjugend' Division and advance elements of the Leibstandarte were thrown into the fray and successfully destroyed a Soviet bridgehead over the River Gran. The main German offensive was launched on 6 March: alongside the four divisions of the Sixth SS Panzer Army (1st, 2nd, 9th and 12th SS Panzer Divisions) were 'Totenkopf' and 'Wiking' and subsequently the 16th SS Panzergrenadier Division – the largest aggregation of SS formations witnessed during the war. At first the SS panzers did well, cutting through the Soviet lines and in places disrupting the Red Army's own offensive plans, but, as ever, the Germans lacked the resources to sustain a full-scale attack and by mid-March their advance had been halted.

As the military initiative of the battle for Hungary passed over to the Red Army so Hitler demanded that his troops stand firm. In the face of overwhelming odds the SS commanders in the field ignored the Führer's orders and instigated a timely retreat. When the news of this disobedience reached Hitler he flew into a hysterical rage and demanded that the SS troops involved remove their coveted divisional arm bands. Dietrich, the SS army commander, refused to pass on the order though, and disillusioned by Hitler's behavior he was reported to have returned his medals and decorations to Hitler in a chamber pot! The failure of the SS in Hungary, following on from the collapse of the Ardennes offensive, marked the end of Hitler's infatuation with the SS. Hitler had been expecting the impossible from the SS; at times they seemed to work miracles on the battlefield but inevitably they were forced to bow to the weight of superior numbers and equipment.

As the SS divisions in Hungary slowly retreated northward into Austria and finally southern Germany, the last act in the saga was being played out in Berlin itself. Obergruppenführer Felix Steiner had been appointed as commander of the Eleventh Panzer Army at the beginning of the year and had been charged with the task of disrupting the Soviet offensive against Berlin. Steiner's army was an admixture of forces typical of that period of the war but the cutting elements were composed of SS units, namely, the 10th SS Panzer Division 'Frundsberg,' 4th Polizei Panzergrenadier Division, 11th Panzergrenadier Division 'Nordland,' SS Brigade 'Nederland' and SS Kampfgruppe 'Wallonie.' On 16 February the Eleventh Panzer Army tore into the flanks of Marshal Zhukov's army group but after initial good progress the German attack ground to a half. Over the succeeding weeks, Steiner's forces were steadily

Below left: **The NCO leader of an SS flame-thrower team signals caution as they make their way through the ruins of a war-torn city. Equipped with a Flammenwerfer 41 flame thrower, the operator had ten seconds' worth of flame, which would normally be fired in a series of short half-second bursts to a maximum range of 30 meters.**

Above: **SS troops rescue what they can from a burning vehicle in Berlin's Anhalter Station, while Soviet troops close in on the doomed city.**

Above right: **As the massed forces of the Red Army steamrollered their way across Poland and into Germany, the German war machine began to break down. The SS continued to fight on, however, even when overrun and abandoned in isolated pockets.**

Right: **Apart from those units fighting in East Prussia and Pomerania on the Baltic coast, the bulk of the Waffen SS was deployed in Hungary in a hopeless attempt to prevent its vital oil wells from falling into Soviet hands. Here, SS infantrymen use the cover of an embankment in the open grasslands of the Hungarian plain, February 1945.**

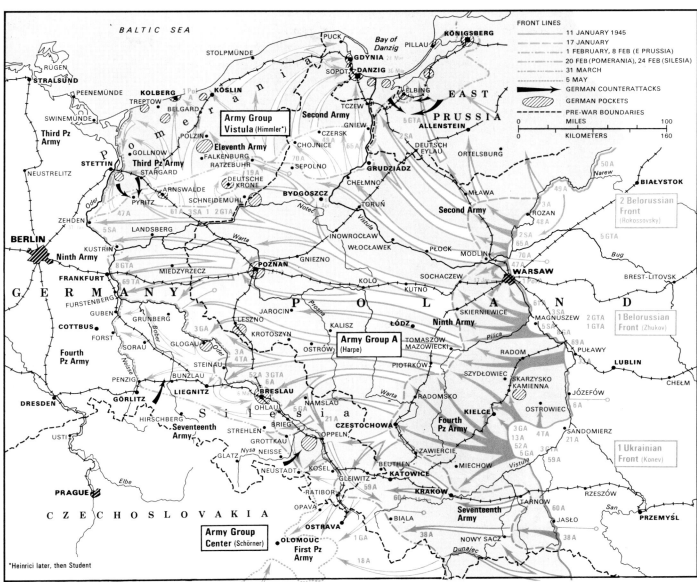

eroded, his units drawn off in desperate 'fire-brigade' operations, so that in the end he described himself as 'a general without any troops.'

Hitler, increasingly isolated in his bunker in Berlin, retreated into a world of fantasy; oblivious to the actual situation above ground he began to order non-existent armies to converge on Berlin in a final masterstroke that, he raved, would crush the Red Army for good. Thus Steiner's Eleventh Panzer Army, which by early April had been reduced to a nucleus of 5000 Luftwaffe personnel and groups of Hitler Youth, became part of Hitler's fantasy world. On 21 April Steiner was ordered to march on Berlin but lacking anything like a sufficient minimum force he awaited upon events. When Hitler was informed of the reality of the situation he flew into a five-hour rage: on the point of hysterical collapse, he declared that his trusted SS had betrayed him, and relieving Steiner of his command (which Steiner ignored) he announced his intention of fighting on alone in Berlin.

Meanwhile, during the last week in April, as the Soviet armies broke into the outer ring of the Berlin defenses, the remaining SS troops carried on the fight as loyally as ever. These remnants of the Waffen SS, fighting only yards away from Hitler's bunker, included elements of the 11th SS Panzergrenadier Division 'Nordland,' 300 French troops from the 33rd Waffen Grenadier Division der SS 'Charlemagne,' a battalion of Latvians from the 15th Waffen Grenadier Division der SS and some 600 men of Himmler's own *Begleitbataillon* (escort battalion). Fighting alongside them were teenagers from the Hitler Youth, and these units battled on in the face of the most hopeless odds. Hitler's suicide on 30 April underscored the hopelessness of the situation, and on 7 April German forces surrendered to the Allies.

The remaining SS units accepted the situation – although there had been calls to continue the struggle underground as part of the 'Werewolf' program – and wherever possible they pushed westward to surrender to the Anglo-American Allies. In contrast to the weary and often dejected columns of Army troops who walked into the PoW cages, the SS maintained a measure of defiance as they were forced into captivity. The SS Standarte 'Deutschland' sent the following radio signal to its divisional headquarters, a message which summed up the Waffen SS fighting spirit: 'The Standarte "Deutschland" – now completely cut off, without supplies, with losses of 70 percent in personnel and equipment, at the end of its strength – must now capitulate. Tomorrow the standarte will march into captivity with all heads held high. The standarte which had the honor of bearing the name "Deutschland" is now signing off.'

Main picture: **SS panzergrenadiers clamber over the imposing bulk of a PzKpfw VI Tiger II, strategically sited on a street corner in the Hungarian capital of Budapest during the summer of 1944. As the Red Army's steamroller advance began to draw near the borders of Hungary, so Hungarian enthusiasm for the Axis cause began to wane: the German military authorities found it expedient to deploy crack troops around Budapest to 'remind' the Hungarians of their treaty obligations.**

Inset picture: **A slightly battered PzKpfw V Panther of the Leibstandarte trundles along the hight street of a Hungarian town.**

Left: **As part of the attempt to rescue the beleaguered German garrison cut-off in Budapest during the winter of 1944-45, SS troops push forward through a wood toward Soviet positions.**

Right: **As the Soviet forces began to tighten their grip on besieged Budapest, the Hungarian Minister for War inspects forward defenses with an SS officer.**

Below: **A fine-looking Arab stallion of the Hungarian Army is led past one of the waiting Tiger IIs under SS control. Commanded by Otto Skorzeny, a select group of SS troops had been infiltrated into Budapest to bring the wavering Hungarian dictator, Admiral Horthy, to heel. Although massively outnumbered, Skorzeny's men adroitly kidnapped Horthy's son and in a brilliant *coup de main* captured Castle Hill, the citadel of Budapest, taking control of the city. Horthy was forced to abdicate and a pro-Nazi regime established.**

Top: '**Commuting' to battle, this SS soldier waits with Hungarian civilians in the center of Budapest for a tram to take him out toward the outer suburbs and the war zone, November 1944. The soldier is armed with a Panzerfaust 60, the lightweight antitank weapon issued to the infantry, capable of penetrating 200mm of armor plate at 60 meters.**

Above: **Despite the best efforts of the Sixth SS Panzer Army to smash its way through the advancing mass of the Red Army, the crack units of the Waffen SS were too exhausted, and numerically too few, to make significant headway. Here, men of the Leibstandarte dismount from their halftracks to inspect a shot-up supply column.**

Right: **An SS halftrack of the 'Wiking' Division stands deserted in the ruins of Berlin, alongside the bodies of its crew. Despite the only too obvious fact that the war was lost the SS continued to fight on, in many cases their ardor for battle undiminished by the hopelessness of their cause. This was particularly true of the many non-German units of the SS: for them surrender would not mean temporary incarceration in a PoW camp; instead they faced the charge of treason and the near certainty of death by firing squad.**

Below: **Alongside the remnants of the SS, the others who carried on the fight regardless of the situation were the teenagers of the Hitler Youth. These young soldiers of the Reich have just been awarded the Iron Cross by the Führer himself (one of his last public appearances at the end of March 1945); the boy in the middle is a 16-year-old named Wilhelm Hübner.**

Right: **A dramatic picture demonstrating the effectiveness of the Panzerfaust – a German soldier has just knocked out a T-34 tank of the Red Army. The Panzerfaust fired a hollow-charge projectile, which detonated a short distance from the enemy tank in order to focus the power of the explosion into a narrow jet to cut through the armor plate.**

Right: **Wearing their special winter parkas two SS soldiers scan a local propaganda broadsheet during a lull in the fighting for the Prussian stronghold of Küstrin, March 1945. As the Soviet armies of Marshal Zhukov closed in on Berlin, German propaganda attempted to draw a parallel with the present situation and that faced by Frederick the Great during the latter stages of the Seven Years' War (1756-63) when Prussia lay at the mercy of the Russian Army: the sudden death of the Russian monarch almost certainly saved Prussia from ignominious defeat, for the new Tsar was an admirer of Frederick and promptly withdrew his forces from the Prussian homeland. This turn of events exercised a magical hold over Hitler but, of course, history was not to repeat itself like that in 1945.**

CONCLUSION

Since the end of the war, old SS veterans and their fellow apologists have fought to exonerate the Waffen SS from the long list of charges brought against it, firstly by distancing the Waffen SS from the other branches of the SS and secondly, by glossing over the war crimes actually committed by Waffen SS units in the field. Despite their claims, the evidence does not bear them out. The relationship between the Waffen SS and other parts of the SS organization was a complex one but personnel were transferred around from one part of the SS to another and in many instances the Waffen SS was employed to support SS police operations, often of a most brutal nature. In addition, scrutiny of the conduct of the Waffen SS on the battlefield reveals repeated examples of atrocities carried out, and then condoned by the Waffen SS High Command.

In contrast to the Army, with its tradition of service going back to Frederick the Great and before, the Waffen SS was a 'modern' institution, embodying the philosophy of National Socialism. Although the vast majority of the SS were not in fact members of the Nazi Party, SS troops were known as the 'political soldiers' of the Reich because of their close association with the Führer and because they seemed to express in military terms the tough, nihilistic warrior image so beloved of the Nazis – men who could take and hand out punishment in equal measure. Many SS officers took such views seriously indeed and this, to a large degree, explains their disregard for what they considered to be quintessentially bourgeois attitudes toward the laws of

Below: **The image ex-members of the Waffen SS prefer to present to the world – defenders of Europe against the 'Bolshevik horde.' Here a PzKpfw VI Tiger tank of the 2nd SS Panzer Division 'Das Reich' moves past Waffen SS troops during the Battle of Kursk, July 1943. That it was Germany who was the aggressor in this conflict, treacherously launching an invasion against an ostensible ally, is conveniently forgotten in this specious reworking of history.**

Above: **A different reality – Waffen SS troops of the Totenkopfverbände are made to dispose of the bodies of their victims following the liberation of Belsen Concentration Camp, April 1945.**

warfare as expressed in agreements like the Geneva Convention. At its most direct, the moral philosophy informing Waffen SS attitudes toward the conduct of war was simple: 'kill or be killed' and 'the strong will inherit the earth.' And while such military Darwinism outraged the sensibilities of Western opponents it certainly helped bind the SS together as an élite fighting force, especially when the war was going against Germany.

That the Waffen SS maintained a consistently high level of battlefield performance throughout the war is not in doubt; testimony from their own comrades-in-arms in the German Army and their opponents in the field – both Soviet and Western – confirms any investigation of their combat record as genuinely first-rate troops. The point that the Waffen SS took away good German soldiers who could have fought as well in the Army – the basic criticism against all élite units – remains valid, but in the case of the Waffen SS its fanatical military philosophy of 'fighting on regardless' made it a bastion of strength when many (though by no means all) Army units began to falter and fade away as the tide of war turned from victory to defeat. The central tragedy of the Waffen SS was that good soldiers were prepared to fight so hard, cause such destruction and suffering, and sacrifice themselves so readily, simply in order to further a psychopath's vision of a world enslaved to his will.

Appendix I
Waffen SS Divisions 1944-45

1st SS Panzer Division Leibstandarte 'Adolf Hitler'
2nd SS Panzer Division 'Das Reich'
3rd SS Panzer Division 'Totenkopf'
4th SS Polizei Panzergrenadier Division
5th SS Panzer Division 'Wiking'
6th SS Gebirgs Division 'Nord'
7th SS Freiwilligen Gebirgs Division 'Prinz Eugen'
8th SS Kavallerie Division 'Florian Geyer'
9th SS Panzer Division 'Frundsberg'
10th SS Panzer Division 'Hohenstaufen'
11th SS Freiwilligen Panzergrenadier Division 'Nordland'
12th SS Panzer Division 'Hitlerjugend'
13th Waffen Gebirgs Division der SS 'Handschar' (kroat Nr.1)
14th Waffen Grenadier Division der SS (galiz Nr.1)
15th Waffen Grenadier Division der SS (lett Nr.1)
16th SS Panzergrenadier Division 'Reichsführer SS'
17th SS Panzergrenadier Division 'Götz von Berlichingen'
18th SS Freiwilligen Panzergrenadier Division 'Horst Wessel'
19th Waffen Grenadier Division der SS (lett Nr.2)
20th Waffen Grenadier Division der SS (estn Nr.1)
*21st Waffen Gebirgs Division der SS 'Skanderbeg' (alban Nr.1)

22nd Freiwilligen Kavallerie Division der SS 'Maria Theresia'
*23rd Waffen Gebirgs Division der SS 'Kama' (kroat Nr.2)[1];
    23rd Freiwilligen Panzergrenadier Division 'Nederland'
*24th Waffen Gebirgs Division der SS 'Karstjäger'
*25th Waffen Grenadier Division der SS 'Hunyadi' (ungar Nr.1)
*26th Waffen Grenadier Division der SS (ungar Nr.2)
*27th SS Freiwilligen Grenadier Division 'Langemarck'
*28th SS Freiwilligen Grenadier Division 'Wallonien'
*29th Waffen Grenadier Division der SS (russ Nr.1)[2]; 29th
    Waffen Grenadier Division der SS (ital Nr.1)
30th Waffen Grenadier Division der SS (russ Nr.2)
*31st SS Freiwilligen Panzergrenadier Division 'Böhmen-Mähren'
*32nd SS Freiwilligen Panzergrenadier Division '30 Januar'
*33rd Waffen Kavallerie Division der SS (ungar Nr.3)[3]; 33rd
    Waffen Grenadier Division 'Charlemagne' (franz Nr.1)
*34th Freiwilligen Grenadier Division 'Landstorm Nederland'
*35th SS Polizei Grenadier Division
*36th Waffen Grenadier Division der SS
*37th SS Freiwilligen Kavallerie Division 'Lützow'
*38th SS Grenadier Division 'Nibelungen'

*Formations that were never at anything like full divisional strength.

[1]The original 23rd Division (kroat Nr.2) was disbanded in late 1944, its numerical designation reassigned to the 'Nederland' Division.
[2]The original 29th Division (russ Nr.1) was transferred to General Vlasov's Russian Liberation Army, its numerical designation reassigned to WGD der SS (ital Nr.1) in April 1945.
[3]The original 33rd Division (ungar Nr.3) was destroyed during the siege of Budapest early in 1945, its numerical designation reassigned to the WGD der SS 'Charlemagne.'

As has been noted above, many of the Waffen SS divisions were never divisions in the numerical sense: some were merely upgraded regiments, or even battalions, while others were just improvised aggregations of stragglers, depot units or reinforcements flung together on the spot and given grandiose divisional titles. Nonetheless this list of Waffen SS field divisions is by no means definitive; apart from a further seven divisions proposed on paper there were many formations and units which existed outside of the main SS divisional organization. Of these the most noteworthy were the two cossack cavalry divisions; the Norwegian ski battalion; 'war bands' from the Balkans and non-Russian areas of the Soviet Union; and the units raised from Indian and British PoWs – although the latter numbered just 58 men.

Appendix II
Comparative Table of Ranks

Waffen SS	German Army	US Army	British Army
Commissioned officers			
Reichsführer SS	Generalfeldmarschall	General of the Army	Field Marshal
SS Oberstgruppenführer	Generaloberst	General	General
SS Obergruppenführer	General		
SS Gruppenführer	Generalleutnant	Lieutenant General	Lieutenant General
SS Brigadeführer	Generalmajor	Major General	Major General
SS Oberführer	—	Brigadier General	Brigadier
SS Standartenführer	Oberst	Colonel	Colonel
SS Obersturmbannführer	Oberstleutnant	Lieutenant Colonel	Lieutenant Colonel
SS Sturmbannführer	Major	Major	Major
SS Hauptsturmführer	Hauptmann	Captain	Captain
SS Obersturmführer	Oberleutnant	1st Lieutenant	Lieutenant
SS Untersturmführer	Leutnant	2nd Lieutenant	2nd Lieutenant
*NCOs and other ranks**			
SS Sturmscharführer	Stabsfeldwebel		
SS Hauptscharführer	Oberfeldwebel		
SS Oberscharführer	Feldwebel		
SS Standartenjunker	Fähnrich		
SS Scharführer	Unterfeldwebel		
SS Unterscharführer	Unteroffizier		
SS Rottenführer	Stabsgefreiter		
	Obergefreiter		
SS Sturmann	Gefreiter		
SS Oberschütze	Oberschütze		
SS Schütze	Schütze		

*Although there is a broad correlation between commissioned officer ranks within most armies, non-commissioned officer ranks vary too much to make direct comparison meaningful. Very roughly 'Gefreiter' ranks compare with those of corporals while the various 'Feldwebel' ranks correspond with those of sergeant, sergeant major, staff sergeant etc.

Appendix III
Strength of Waffen SS, June-July 1941

SS Division LAH	10,796	Inspectorate of Concentration	
SS Division 'Reich'	19,021	Camps	7200
SS Totenkopf Division	18,754	SS Guard Battalions	2159
SS Polizei Division	17,347	SS Garrison Posts	992
SS Division 'Wiking'	19,377	SS Officer and NCO Schools	1028
SS Division 'Nord'	10,573	SS Volunteer Battalion 'Nordost'	904
Kommandostab RFSS	18,438		
Administrative Department	4007	Total 160,405	
Reserve Units	29,809		

Appendix IV
Organization of SS Panzer Divisions

The division was the basic 'counting block' of the armies of World War II, especially so as the division was the smallest formation capable of independent action, being equipped with a strong infantry component and a full range of supporting arms and services. Organization and strength of a division varied according to its intended role, whether, for example, it was an infantry, cavalry, panzer, airborne or mountain division. Of all these various types the most powerful was the panzer division.

During the course of the war panzer divisions decreased in size but this was compensated for by an increase in firepower through more powerful supporting arms. In the period leading up to D-Day a typical SS panzer division would be organized, armed and equipped as follows. At the heart of the division was the panzer regiment comprising two battalions, one equipped with PzKpfw V Panther tanks, the other with the older PzKpfw IVs. Each battalion would have around 60 tanks and the combined strength of the regiment would be approximately 2400 men. Alongside the panzer regiment were the two panzergrenadier regiments, each of 3300 men and as fully motorized units they were equipped with over 500 vehicles each. In keeping with the German policy of integrating its artillery support at all levels, each regiment was assigned 18 pieces of field artillery, 24 flame throwers and 12 heavy mortars. The divisional artillery regiment (2500 men) fielded a formidable array of ordnance: 12 × 17cm gun/howitzers, 6 × 15cm gun/howitzers, 12 × 10.5cm self-propelled guns, and 12 × 10.5cm gun/howitzers. Supporting these major units were the panzerjäger battalion (31 self-propelled guns); reconnaissance battalion (13 self-propelled guns, 35 × 2cm Pak guns, over 1000 men strong); pioneer battalion (over 1000 men strong); signals battalion; Flak battalion (12 × 8.8cm and 18 × 2cm AA guns); StuG battalion (30 StuG III/IVs); and finally a Nebelwerfer battalion (18 Nebelwerfer rocket launchers).

Bibliographical Note

The two best general histories of the Waffen SS remain Gerald R Reitlinger's *The SS: Alibi of a Nation 1922-1945* (Arms and Armor Press, 1981), which, however, covers all aspects of the SS, and George H Stein's *The Waffen SS: Hitler's Elite Guard at War 1939-1945* (Cornell University Press, 1984). The number of illustrated books on the Waffen SS has increased steadily over the years and cover most aspects of the subject. Among these are three volumes by Bruce Quarrie, published by Patrick Stephens Limited: *Hitler's Samurai: The Waffen SS in Action* (1986), *Hitler's Teutonic Knights: SS Panzers in Action* (1986), and *Weapons and Equipment of the Waffen SS* (1988). Other similar books include: *Waffen SS* (Blanford Press) by Brian Davis; *Waffen SS* (Osprey, 1982) by Martin Windrow; *A Pictorial History of the SS 1923-1945* (Macdonald and Janes, 1976) by Andrew Mollo; and *Waffen SS: The Asphalt Soldiers* (Ballantine, 1970) by John Keegan.

Since the 1960s German publishers have issued a series of German-language, multi-volume histories of specific divisions, which while covering their subject in exhaustive detail are still little more than anodyne apologias for the conduct of the Waffen SS. In English there is *Hitler's Elite: Leibstandarte 1939-1945* (Macdonald and Janes, 1975) by James Lucas and Matthew Cooper, and Max Hastings' *Das Reich* (Michael Joseph, 1981), the latter a detailed study of the events surrounding the Oradour atrocity. On this subject, Robin Mackness' *Oradour: Massacre and Aftermath* (Bloomsbury, 1988) suggests an intriguingly different motivation behind the killings.

Index

Acknowledgments

The publisher and author would like to thank Adrian Hodgkins for the book's design and Ron Watson for compiling the index. We would also like to thank the following picture agencies, institutions and individuals for supplying the illustrations on the pages noted:

Archiv für Kunst und Geschichte, pages: 1, 12, 13, 138(Bottom),

Archiv Gerstenberg, pages: 26(Bottom), 32(Bottom), 37(Top), 56(Top), 86(Bottom), 91(Top), 93(top), 95(Bottom), 107(Bottom Right), 115(Bottom), 116, 120(Bottom), 123(Bottom), 125(Top), 126(Top), 127(Bottom), 128(Top), 139(Top Right), 145(Bottom Left),

Bison Books, pages: 2, 3, 4, 6-7, 15, 16(Bottom), 18(Bottom), 26(Top), 39(Top), 65(Both), 66(Right), 68-69, 69(Top), 76, 88, 89(Top), 137(Top Both), 140, 144, 145(Bottom Right), 148, 173(Bottom),

Bundesarchiv, pages: 10, 16(Top), 18(Top), 19(Bottom), 27(Top), 36(Bottom), 40-41(Top), 48(Bottom), 97(Both), 118(Top), 128(Bottom), 138(Top), 139(Top Left), 155(Both), 156(Bottom), 168(Top), 180-181(Main), 183(Top Right), 184(Bottom),

Collection B L Davis, pages: 20-21, 22(Both), 23(Both), 24(Bottom), 35(Bottom), 41(Bottom), 47(Top), 49(Bottom), 58(Top & Bottom), 59(Top), 64(Top), 67(Both), 69(Bottom), 74, 75(Bottom), 77(Top), 78, 79(All 3), 82(All 3), 84(Top), 86(Top), 87(Left), 88(Both), 89(Bottom), 90(Both), 91(Bottom), 92, 94, 98(Left), 99(Both), 100(Top), 101, 102(Bottom), 104(Bottom), 105(Both), 106(Top Both), 108-109, 109(Top), 123(Top Both), 124(Top), 127(Top), 129(Top), 130(Bottom Left), 131(Bottom), 132-133(Bottom), 133(Top), 134(Both), 135(Both), 142(Both), 143(Both), 145(Top), 150(Bottom), 154(Bottom Both),

162(Top), 163(Bottom), 165(Right), 167(Top), 178(Bottom), 183(Top Left),

Robert Hunt Library, pages: 14(Bottom), 24(Top), 34(Top), 35(Top), 38, 38-39, 39(Bottom), 40(Both), 42(Top & Bottom Left), 43(Both), 44(Both), 45(All 3), 46(Both), 49(Top & Middle), 58(Middle), 59(Bottom), 61, 62(Right), 63(Both), 64(Bottom), 66(Right), 70(Both), 71(Top), 72(Bottom), 80, 81(Bottom), 84(Bottom), 85(Both), 87(Right), 93(Bottom), 96-97, 100(Bottom), 102(Top), 103(Both), 104(Top), 106(Bottom), 107(Top), 110(Both), 111(Top), 118(Bottom), 120(Top & Middle), 121(Bottom), 122, 124(Bottom), 125(Bottom), 129(Bottom), 130(Bottom Right), 131(Top), 132(Both), 135(Top), 156(Top), 156-157(Bottom), 157, 158(Both), 159(Bottom), 160(Both), 161(Both), 162(Bottom Both), 164(Both), 165(Left), 167(Bottom), 170(Bottom), 173(Top), 174(Top), 175(Top), 178(Top), 180-181(Inset),

182(Both), 183(Bottom), 186,

Imperial War Museum, London, pages: 11, 17(All 3), 25(Top), 31, 32(Top), 33, 42(Bottom Right), 47(Bottom), 48(Top), 52, 73, 111(Bottom), 115(Top), 117, 119(Top), 126(Bottom), 139(Bottom), 141, 150(Top), 153, 166, 168(Bottom Both), 169(Both), 170(Top), 171(All 3), 172(Both), 174(Bottom), 175(Bottom), 187,

Library of Congress, pages: 54-55, 151,

Peter Newark's Military Pictures, pages: 34(Bottom), 107(Bottom Left), 136, 137(Bottom 2), 185(Top),

Orbis Publishing Ltd, pages: 52-53, 56(Bottom), 81(Top), 83(Top), 95(Top), 98-99(Top), 152-153, 163(Top),

US National Archives, pages: 14(Top), 19(Top), 159(Top).